"Swami Sweeji"

Krishna Jkhetani

Grade 2

Home Book

ZB
SPELLING
CONNECTIONS

J. Richard Gentry, Ph.D.

3

Series Author
J. Richard Gentry, Ph.D.

Editorial Development: Cottage Communications

Art and Production: PC&F

Photography: George C. Anderson: cover; pages 1, 4, 6, 7, 254, 255, 256, 257

Illustrations: Laurel Aiello: pages 34, 45, 63, 70, 94, 99, 224, 225, 227, 228, 231, 232, 233, 236, 237, 238, 240, 241, 242, 243, 244, 245, 247, 249, 250, 251, 252, 253; Dave Blanchette: pages 10, 13, 22, 23, 173, 195, 197, 234; Nan Brooks: pages 166, 178, 179; Tom Elliot: pages 31, 72; Rusty Fletcher: pages 125, 207, 209, 215; Collin Fry: pages 16, 28; Kate Gorman: pages 136, 142, 154, 159, 196; Shana Greger: pages 39, 40, 41, 42, 74, 75, 76, 77, 78, 111, 112, 114, 147, 148, 149, 150, 183, 184, 185, 186, 219, 220, 221, 222; Steve Henry: pages 27, 52, 57, 59, 87, 117, 119, 143, 155, 160, 191; Bill Ogden: pages 11, 17, 19, 21, 33, 35, 46, 47, 51, 58, 64, 65, 69, 71, 81, 89, 93, 95, 100, 101, 106, 118, 124, 137, 167, 177, 190, 201, 214; Vickie Woodworth: pages 29, 53, 61, 83, 107, 153, 161, 172, 203, 208

The following references were used in the development of the **Word Study** activities included on the **Vocabulary Connections** pages in each developmental spelling unit:

Ayto, John. *Arcade Dictionary of Word Origins: The Histories of More Than 8,000 English-Language Words.* New York: Arcade Publishing, Little, Brown, and Company, 1990.

Barnhart, Robert K., ed. *The Barnhart Dictionary of Etymology: The Core Vocabulary of Standard English.* New York: The H.W. Wilson Company, 1988.

Makkai, Adam, ed. *A Dictionary of American Idioms.* New York: Barron's Educational Series, Inc., 1987.

Rheingold, Howard. *They Have a Word for It: A Lighthearted Lexicon of Untranslatable Words and Phrases.* Los Angeles: Jeremy P. Tarcher, Inc., 1988.

Terban, Marvin. *Time to Rhyme: A Rhyming Dictionary.* Honesdale, PA: Wordsong, Boyds Mills Press, 1994.

ISBN: 0-7367-2068-5

Copyright © 2004 Zaner-Bloser, Inc.

Zaner-Bloser, Inc., P.O. Box 16764, Columbus, Ohio 43216-6764 (1-800-421-3018)
www.zaner-bloser.com
Printed in the United States of America   06 07 (104) 5

Contents

Spelling Study Strategy

Look ➡ **Say** ➡ Cover ➡ **See** ➡ **Write** ➡ Check

1 **Look** at the word.

2 **Say** the letters in the word. Think about how each sound is spelled.

3 **Cover** the word with your hand or close your eyes.

4 **See** the word in your mind. Spell the word to yourself.

5 **Write** the word.

6 **Check** your spelling against the spelling in the book.

Spelling and Thinking

READ THE SPELLING WORDS

1. land	*land*	The farmer planted corn on his **land**.
2. stick	*stick*	Kayla used a big **stick** as a bat.
3. plan	*plan*	Dad will help us **plan** our vacation.
4. trip	*trip*	Our class went on a **trip** to the zoo.
5. stand	*stand*	Please **stand** in this line.
6. act	*act*	My sister likes to **act** in plays.
7. thing	*thing*	What is that **thing** on your desk?
8. last	*last*	John spent his **last** dollar on pizza.
9. lift	*lift*	This box is too heavy to **lift**.
10. band	*band*	The **band** plays music at games.
11. grand	*grand*	Lisa won the **grand** prize.
12. swim	*swim*	Shana likes to **swim** in the pool.
13. stamp	*stamp*	Please put a **stamp** on this letter.
14. list	*list*	Write the words in a short **list**.
15. sand	*sand*	Many beaches are covered by **sand**.

SORT THE SPELLING WORDS

Each word on the spelling list has the **short a** sound or the **short i** sound.

1.–9. Write the words that have the **short a** sound.

10.–15. Write the words that have the **short i** sound.

REMEMBER THE SPELLING STRATEGY

Remember that the **short a** sound you hear in **plan** is spelled **a**. The **short i** sound you hear in **trip** is spelled **i**.

8

Spelling and Phonics

Ending Sounds

1.–5. Write the spelling words that rhyme with **and**. Circle the consonant cluster at the end of each rhyming word.

Word Structure

6. Change the first letter of **fast** to make this spelling word.

7. Change the first letter of **mist** to make this spelling word.

8. Change the first two letters of **sting** to make this spelling word.

Sound and Letter Patterns

9.–10. Write spelling words by adding the missing letters.

sw___m   st___ck

11.–15. The words in a dictionary are in a-b-c order. Look at the first letter of each word below. Write these words in a-b-c order.

plan   trip   lift   act   stamp

◆ ◆ ◆

Dictionary Check Be sure to check the a-b-c order of the words in your **Spelling Dictionary**.

Spelling and Reading

land	stick	plan	trip	stand
act	thing	last	lift	band
grand	swim	stamp	list	sand

Solve the Analogies Write a spelling word to complete each analogy.

1. **Beginning** is to **first** as **end** is to _____.
2. **Ship** is to **water** as **car** is to _____.
3. **Song** is to **sing** as **play** is to _____.
4. **Worm** is to **crawl** as **fish** is to _____.
5. **Small** is to **tiny** as **large** is to _____.

Complete the Meanings Write the spelling word that fits each clue.

6. Taylor likes to _____ on her head.
7. Pablo can _____ the large stone.
8. This postcard needs a _____.
9. Throw this dry _____ on the fire.
10. Kim plays drums in a _____.

Complete the Story Write the spelling words from the box to complete the story.

After school let out, the Lee family decided to
__11.__ a vacation. Kim and Nucha made a
__12.__ of places they wanted to visit. They each
wrote down one __13.__ they hoped to do. All of
the Lees wanted to build castles of __14.__. Where
do you think the Lees will go on their __15.__?

sand
plan
trip
thing
list

Spelling and Writing

Proofread a Letter

Five words are not spelled correctly in this letter.
Write the words correctly.

Dear Parents:

   Come clean up the lan of Grand Park with us.
Our class will take a tripp there on October 15.
You can pick up each big stik and left up every
heavy think. We hope you can come at 10 o'clock.

                    Mr. Bell's Third Grade Class

Proofreading Marks

≡   Make a capital.
/   Make a small letter.
∧   Add something.
℮   Take out something.
⊙   Add a period.
New paragraph
SP Spelling error

Write a Letter

Persuasive Writing

Pretend that your class is cleaning up a park. Write a
letter to your parents and ask them to help. Be sure to
give all of the information they need, such as

- the name of the park
- when the cleanup takes place
- what you plan to do to clean up the park
- what kind of help you need from grown-ups

Write a rough draft of your letter first. Use as many
spelling words as you can.

Proofread Your Writing During

Proofread your writing for spelling errors. Be sure to use
a dictionary to check the spelling if you are not sure.

Writing Process

Prewriting
⇩
Drafting
⇩
Revising
⇩
Editing
⇩
Publishing

VOCABULARY CONNECTIONS

►Strategy Words◄

Review Words: Short a, Short i

Write a word from the box to complete each sentence.

bat	fan	miss	win

1. People use a _____ to keep cool on warm summer days and nights.
2. If you _____ the bus, you can walk to school.
3. Eric got a ball and a _____ for his birthday.
4. The best speller will _____ the spelling bee in our class.

Preview Words: Short a, Short i

Write a word from the box that matches each clue.

brick	dancer	gadget	skill

5. Any small kitchen tool can be called this.
6. The Big Bad Wolf could not blow down the house built of this.
7. If you are this, you move your body to the rhythm of the music.
8. A writer needs this to write well.

Content Words

Math: Numbers

Write the word from the box that is the answer.

| fifteen | sixteen | seventeen | eighteen |

1. six + ten = _____
2. eight + ten = _____
3. five + ten = _____
4. seven + ten = _____

Science: Trees

Write the name of each leaf.

| oak | maple | elm | birch |

5. o____
6. e____
7. m____
8. b____

Apply the Spelling Strategy

Circle the two Content Words you wrote that contain the **short i** sound.

Word Study

More Than One Meaning

Write the one Strategy Word that fits both of these meanings:

- something that moves air for cooling
- someone who really likes something a lot

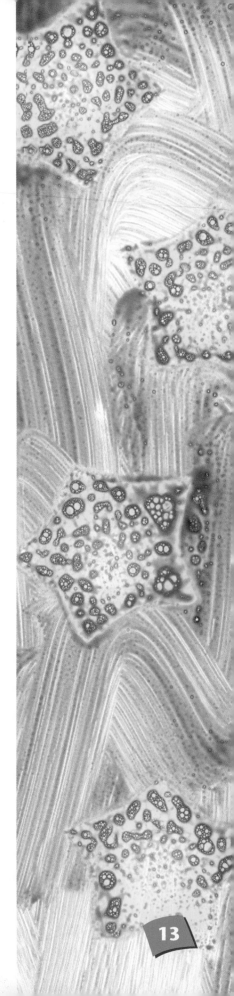

Spelling and Thinking

1. crop	*crop*	Ms. Lutz is harvesting her bean **crop**.
2. test	*test*	Joni passed her spelling **test**.
3. clock	*clock*	Is the time on this **clock** correct?
4. spent	*spent*	Dana **spent** her lunch money on candy.
5. drop	*drop*	Ben felt a **drop** of rain on his head.
6. left	*left*	Mary writes with her **left** hand.
7. sled	*sled*	The **sled** slid on the ice.
8. plot	*plot*	He grows peas in his garden **plot**.
9. spend	*spend*	Juan and Shawn **spend** summers at camp.
10. west	*west*	The sun sets in the **west**.
11. block	*block*	He carved a dog from a **block** of wood.
12. tent	*tent*	Lions rode on horses in the circus **tent**.
13. desk	*desk*	Shanita likes to study at her **desk**.
14. flock	*flock*	The **flock** of birds flew south in the fall.
15. nest	*nest*	The crow laid an egg in its **nest**.

SORT THE SPELLING WORDS

1.–6. Write the words that have the **short o** sound spelled **o**.

7.–15. Write the words that have the **short e** sound spelled **e**.

REMEMBER THE SPELLING STRATEGY

Remember that the **short o** sound you hear in **drop** is spelled **o**. The **short e** sound you hear in **desk** is spelled **e**.

Spelling ^{and} Phonics

Ending Sounds —————————————————

1.–3. Write the spelling words that rhyme with **rock**. Circle the two consonants at the end of each word.

4.–5. Write the spelling words that rhyme with **went**. Circle the two consonants at the end of each word.

Word Structure —————————————————

6. Replace the first letter of **bend** with two consonants to make this spelling word.

7. Replace the vowel in **drip** to make this word.

Sound and Letter Patterns —————————

8.–10. Write spelling words by adding the missing letters.

cr__p   de__k   plo__

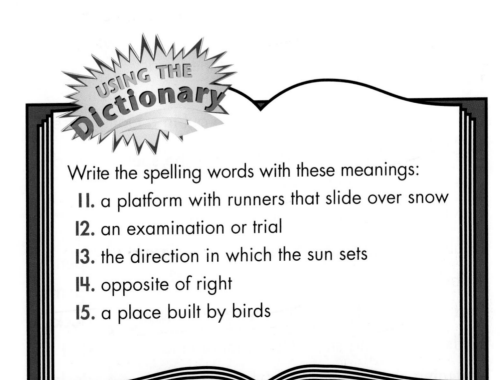

Write the spelling words with these meanings:

11. a platform with runners that slide over snow

12. an examination or trial

13. the direction in which the sun sets

14. opposite of right

15. a place built by birds

Spelling and Reading

crop	test	clock	spent	drop
left	sled	plot	spend	west
block	tent	desk	flock	nest

Complete the Rhymes Read each sentence below. Write a spelling word to complete each rhyme.

1. I did my very <u>best</u> and scored a 100 on my _____.

2. The henhouse had a <u>theft</u>. Only a few eggs were _____.

3. The skunk looked east, then north and south. Finally the <u>pest</u> ran _____.

Replace the Words Write the spelling word that could best replace each underlined word or words.

4. He carved a horse from a <u>solid piece</u> of wood.

5. The <u>group</u> of birds flew south for the winter.

6. That farmer's main <u>plant</u> is corn.

7. Please <u>leave</u> off the books at the library.

8. This <u>section</u> of land will make a good garden.

9. My friends and I like to camp out in a <u>cloth house</u>.

Complete the Paragraph Write the spelling word that belongs in each blank.

Many people __10.__ time enjoying hobbies. My grandfather builds things from wood. Last year he built a __11.__, a __12.__, and a __13.__. My grandmother likes to watch birds. This spring she __14.__ a lot of time watching some robins build their __15.__.

nest
spend
spent
clock
sled
desk

16

Spelling and Writing

Proofread a Journal Entry

Five words are not spelled correctly in this journal entry. Write the words correctly.

> September 10
>
> Amy and I went camping. When we got to the camp, we first set up our tint. Next we spint some time fishing. Then we watched a flok of geese eat grass. We didn't see a nest. Before we went to sleep, I told a story with a scary plott. Finally we set our cluck to get up early the next day.

Proofreading Marks

≡	Make a capital.
/	Make a small letter.
∧	Add something.
ℓ	Take out something.
⊙	Add a period.
⌗	New paragraph
(SP)	Spelling error

Write a Journal Entry

Narrative Writing

Write a journal entry about anything you wish, such as
- something you did today.
- something exciting that happened at school.
- something that happened on the way to school.

Begin the rough draft by writing today's date. In your entry, tell what happened first, what happened next, what happened after that, and what happened last. Use as many spelling words as you can.

Proofread Your Writing During

Proofread your writing for spelling errors. Be sure to use a dictionary to check the spelling if you are not sure.

Writing Process

Prewriting
⇩
Drafting
⇩
Revising
⇩
Editing
⇩
Publishing

Unit 2 enrichment

▸Strategy Words◂

Review Words: Short o, Short e

Write a word from the box to complete each sentence.

cot	nod	send	tell

1. Please _____ me again what you need from the store.
2. Eric sleeps on a _____ when he stays at my house.
3. I will _____ you a postcard from camp.
4. Did you _____ your head?

Preview Words: Short o, Short e

Write a word from the box that matches each clue.

colony	kept	letters	socket

5. The first English settlers created this in America in 1607.
6. This can hold a plug or a light bulb.
7. Your friends might send you these if you move to a new home.
8. If you did not return something, you probably did this with it.

18

Content Words

Science: Birds

Write the name of each bird.

| crow | hawk | owl | robin |

1.
2.
3.
4.

Language Arts: Past-Tense Verbs

Write the past-tense verb that fits each sentence.

| slept | slid | swam | sang |

5. The car _____ on the ice.
6. The boy _____ in the pool.
7. She _____ the song as loud as she could.
8. The bear _____ in its den until spring.

Apply the Spelling Strategy

Circle the Content Word you wrote that has the **short o** sound. Underline the Content Word you wrote that has the **short e** sound.

Word Study

Make a New Word

You can use a word chain to make a new word. Change the letter in dark type in each word, in order, to make a new word. Write the Strategy Word that completes this word chain: le**f**t, le**n**t, **l**end, _____.

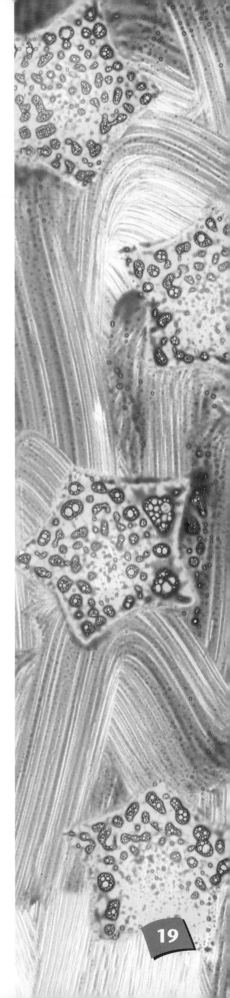

19

Spelling ᴬⁿᵈ Thinking

READ THE SPELLING WORDS

1. lunch	*lunch*	Domingo ate **lunch** at noon.
2. until	*until*	We stroked the cat **until** it purred.
3. cover	*cover*	What is on the **cover** of your book?
4. buzz	*buzz*	Tamika heard some bees **buzz**.
5. become	*become*	Joel wants to **become** a teacher.
6. stuff	*stuff*	We will **stuff** the old pillow.
7. nothing	*nothing*	The gift she made cost **nothing**.
8. dull	*dull*	We can shine up these **dull** coins.
9. month	*month*	February is the shortest **month**.
10. study	*study*	People **study** to learn.
11. love	*love*	Karen has a **love** for pets.
12. uncle	*uncle*	An **uncle** is a parent's brother.
13. cuff	*cuff*	The **cuff** of the sleeve was dirty.
14. none	*none*	She ate the apples and left us **none**.
15. under	*under*	Is the baseball **under** the bed again?

SORT THE SPELLING WORDS

1.–9. Write the words that spell the **short u** sound **u**.

10.–15. Write the words that spell the **short u** sound **o**.

REMEMBER THE SPELLING STRATEGY

Remember that the **short u** sound can be spelled in different ways: **u** in **lunch** and **o** in **become**.

Spelling and Phonics

Beginning Sounds

1.–3. Write the spelling words that begin with the **short u** sound.

Sound and Letter Patterns

4.–7. Write the spelling words that end with two consonants that are the same. Circle the two consonants.

8.–9. Write the one-syllable spelling words that end with two different consonants that work together to spell one sound. Circle the two consonants.

Word Structure

10. Replace the first two letters in **diver** to make a spelling word.

11. Add one letter to **one** to make a spelling word.

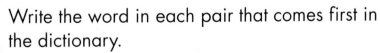

USING THE Dictionary

Write the word in each pair that comes first in the dictionary.

12. uncle, study

13. become, buzz

14. nothing, under

15. lunch, love

◆ ◆ ◆

Dictionary Check Be sure to check the a-b-c order of the words in your **Spelling Dictionary**.

Spelling and Reading

lunch	until	cover	buzz	become
stuff	nothing	dull	month	study
love	uncle	cuff	none	under

Solve the Analogies Write a spelling word to complete each analogy.

1. **Dog** is to **bark** as **bee** is to _____.
2. **Night** is to **day** as **sharp** is to _____.
3. **Out** is to **in** as **over** is to _____.
4. **Mother** is to **father** as **aunt** is to _____.
5. **Morning** is to **breakfast** as **noon** is to _____.
6. **Game** is to **practice** as **test** is to _____.
7. **Ten** is to **zero** as **many** is to _____.

Complete the Sentences Write the spelling word that belongs in each sentence.

8. Latoya's birthday is next _____.
9. Rob sewed a button on the _____ of his shirt.
10. Babies _____ being cuddled.

Complete the Story Write the spelling words from the box to complete the story.

Dave has ___11.___ fond of his new black shoes. He lost one shoe and did not want to go to school ___12.___ he found it. Under his dresser he found socks, toys, and lots of other ___13.___ but no shoe. There was ___14.___ at all under his bed. Finally, he lifted the ___15.___ off his bed and there it was!

| nothing |
| until |
| cover |
| become |
| stuff |

Spelling and Writing

Proofread a Paragraph

Five words are not spelled correctly in this paragraph. Write the words correctly.

My best friend and I ate lonch in the park. Then we went home and played games untill three. Afterward, we had to stody. Sometimes we do nothin but sit and talk undr a maple tree. That is fun, too. We love to be together.

Proofreading Marks

≡	Make a capital.
/	Make a small letter.
∧	Add something.
ℓ	Take out something.
⊙	Add a period.
⌗	New paragraph
SP	Spelling error

Write a Paragraph

Narrative Writing

Write a paragraph about some things you did with a friend. Take these steps before you begin:

- Make a list of things or activities you do that are fun.
- Choose one thing to write about.
- Write down some words to remind you of what you want to include in your paragraph.
- Write a rough draft of the paragraph using your notes.

Use as many spelling words as you can.

Proofread Your Writing During

Proofread your writing for spelling errors. Be sure to use a dictionary to check the spelling if you are not sure.

Writing Process

Prewriting
⇩
Drafting
⇩
Revising
⇩
Editing
⇩
Publishing

Strategy Words

Review Words: Short u

Write the word from the box to complete each sentence.

cup	dust	jump	rub

1. Mica drank milk from the _____.
2. Did you see the tiger _____ its back against the tree?
3. I like to help my father _____ the furniture.
4. My cat likes to _____ on the top of the table.

Preview Words: Short u

Write a word from the box that matches each meaning.

button	hunter	summit	trust

5. the highest point of something
6. an animal who chases another animal for food
7. a round object that fastens clothes together
8. belief in another

24

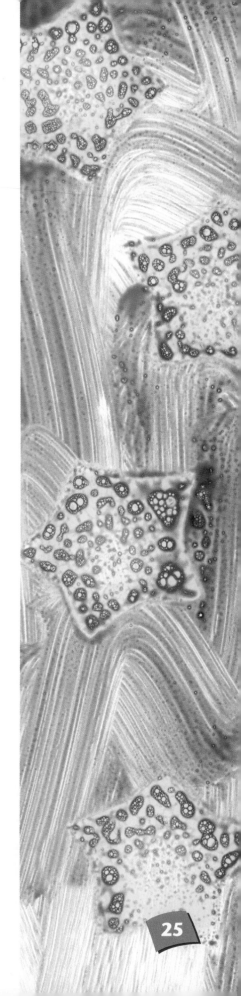

Content Words

Science: Beekeeping

Write the word from the box that fits each blank.

| bees | clover | honey | beeswax |

The ___1.___ gather nectar from flowers and make ___2.___. The wax made by the bees to build their honeycombs is called ___3.___. You might see bees gathering nectar in a field of ___4.___.

Language Arts: Onomatopoeia

Write the word from the box that names the sound each of these might make.

| hiss | click | bang | beep |

5. a snake
6. a car horn

7. a slamming door
8. horse's hoofs

Apply the Spelling Strategy

Circle the letter that spells the **short u** sound in one of the Content Words you wrote.

Suffixes

The **-er** suffix can be added to a verb to name a person who does something. For example, a **baker** is someone who bakes. Write the Strategy Word that has the **-er** suffix and means "a person who hunts."

Spelling and Thinking

READ THE SPELLING WORDS

1. proud	*proud*	I am **proud** of myself for getting an A.
2. boil	*boil*	Water will **boil** when it gets very hot.
3. loud	*loud*	The music was too **loud** for my ears.
4. house	*house*	The Carters live in a large **house**.
5. join	*join*	Roberto wants to **join** the scouts.
6. cloud	*cloud*	We saw a dark **cloud** in the sky.
7. sound	*sound*	The loud ringing **sound** made me jump.
8. voice	*voice*	The singer had a beautiful **voice**.
9. oil	*oil*	Fish is often fried in **oil**.
10. round	*round*	Put the cake batter in the **round** pan.
11. point	*point*	Please sharpen the **point** of this pencil.
12. south	*south*	North is the opposite of **south**.
13. found	*found*	Tamika **found** her lost money.
14. soil	*soil*	Some plants need rich **soil** to grow well.
15. ground	*ground*	It is hard to dig in the frozen **ground**.

SORT THE SPELLING WORDS

Each word on the spelling list has the vowel sound in **oil** or in **loud**.

1.–6. Write the words that have the /**oi**/ sound.
7.–15. Write the words that have the /**ou**/ sound.

REMEMBER THE SPELLING STRATEGY

Remember that the /**oi**/ sound you hear in **oil** is spelled **oi**. The /**ou**/ sound you hear in **loud** is spelled **ou**.

26

Spelling ᵃⁿᵈ Phonics

Rhyming Words _____

1.–3. Write **oil** and the spelling words that rhyme with **oil**.

4.–6. Write **loud** and the spelling words that rhyme with **loud**. Circle the words you wrote that begin with a consonant cluster.

7.–10. Write **sound** and the spelling words that rhyme with **sound**. Circle the word you wrote that begins with a consonant cluster.

Word Structure _____

11. Change one letter in **mouse** to make a spelling word.

12. Change one letter in **paint** to make a spelling word.

13. Change one letter in **mouth** to make a spelling word.

USING THE Dictionary

14. Write the spelling word that would come last in the dictionary.

15. Write the spelling word that would come after **house** but before **loud** in the dictionary.

◆ ◆ ◆

Dictionary Check Be sure to check your answers in your **Spelling Dictionary**.

Spelling and Reading

proud	boil	loud	house	join
cloud	sound	voice	oil	round
point	south	found	soil	ground

Solve the Analogies   Write a spelling word to complete each analogy.

1. **Box** is to **square** as **ball** is to _____.
2. **East** is to **west** as **north** is to _____.
3. **Whisper** is to **quiet** as **yell** is to _____.
4. **Cold** is to **freeze** as **hot** is to _____.
5. **Find** is to **found** as **grind** is to _____.

Replace the Words   Write the spelling word that could best replace each underlined word or words.

6. Shall we study at my <u>home</u>?
7. The teacher's <u>tone</u> was cheerful.
8. He wants to <u>become a member of</u> the math club.

Complete the Paragraph   Write the spelling words from the box that complete the paragraph.

sound	point	oil	proud	found	soil	cloud

   Judy Kane was __9.__ to be the Science Fair winner. Her model showed how rainwater goes from a __10.__ in the sky, to the earth, and back again. She used arrows to __11.__ to the water soaking into some sandy __12.__. She rubbed salad __13.__ on the grass to make it look wet. She even __14.__ a way to make the __15.__ of rain!

28

Spelling and Writing

 Proofread an Article ———————————————

Five words are not spelled correctly in this article. Write the words correctly.

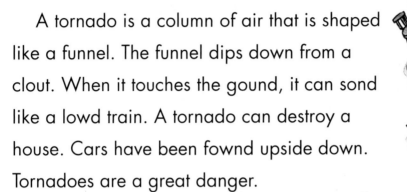

A tornado is a column of air that is shaped like a funnel. The funnel dips down from a clout. When it touches the gound, it can sond like a lowd train. A tornado can destroy a house. Cars have been fownd upside down. Tornadoes are a great danger.

Proofreading Marks

≡ Make a capital.

/ Make a small letter.

∧ Add something.

ℓ Take out something.

⊙ Add a period.

⌗ New paragraph

SP Spelling error

Write an Article ———————— *Expository Writing*

Write an article about a thunderstorm, snowstorm, or another kind of storm. The information must be true. Before you start writing, fold a sheet of paper into three columns to list your ideas. Label each column with one of these headings:

• See   • Hear   • Feel

Include the information in your columns as you write your article. Use as many spelling words as you can.

Writing Process

Prewriting

⇩

Drafting

⇩

Revising

⇩

Proofread Your Writing During ► **Editing**

⇩

Publishing

Proofread your writing for spelling errors. Be sure to check each word carefully. Use a dictionary to check spelling if you are not sure.

29

Strategy Words

Review Words: ou, oi

Write a word from the box to complete each sentence.

bounce	coin	count	shout

1. He had trouble hearing me in the storm, so I had to _____.
2. Did you _____ the number of stars in the flag?
3. We watched the ball _____ across the street.
4. The _____ slipped through a small hole in my pocket.

Preview Words: ou, oi

Write a word from the box that matches each clue.

aloud	choice	mouth	noise

5. The dentist often asks you to open this wide to check your teeth.
6. If you read a book this way, everyone can hear you.
7. You have this if you can pick something.
8. This is the name of a loud sound.

30

Content Words

Science: Weather

Write the word that completes each sentence.

| weather | sunny | cloudy | hail |

1. When it snows or storms, people say that the _____ is bad.
2. Ice that falls from the sky is called _____.
3. When the sun does not shine, the day is _____.
4. It hardly ever rains on a _____ day.

Math: Ordinal Numbers

Look at the picture. Write the word from the box that completes each sentence.

| fifth | seventh | sixth | eighth |

5. The clown is _____ in line.
6. The boy with the airplane is _____ in line.
7. The girl holding the ball is _____ in line.
8. The man in the blue shirt is _____ in line.

Apply the Spelling Strategy

Circle the Content Word you wrote that contains the /**ou**/ sound.

Line starts here.

Word Study

Spelling Changes Over Time

Long ago this Content Word was spelled **weder**. Later, the **d** was changed to **th**. Write the word.

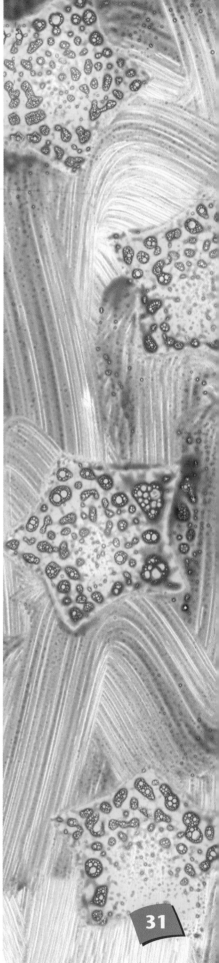

Spelling and Thinking

READ THE SPELLING WORDS

1.	crew	*crew*	A **crew** of workers fixed the street.
2.	loose	*loose*	His **loose** baby tooth fell out.
3.	news	*news*	The good **news** is that he won the race.
4.	school	*school*	Kurt left his books at **school**.
5.	drew	*drew*	Shandra **drew** a picture of Alex.
6.	knew	*knew*	She **knew** that lying was wrong.
7.	smooth	*smooth*	The shirt felt **smooth** and soft.
8.	pool	*pool*	He swam in the deep **pool**.
9.	shoot	*shoot*	Can I **shoot** a picture of you?
10.	threw	*threw*	Michael **threw** the garbage out.
11.	roof	*roof*	A worker fixed the leaking **roof**.
12.	fool	*fool*	The clown acted like a silly **fool**.
13.	chew	*chew*	She asked us to **chew** our food slowly.
14.	balloon	*balloon*	The **balloon** floated into the sky.
15.	choose	*choose*	We will **choose** a color for the walls.

SORT THE SPELLING WORDS

1.–6. Write the words that have the /oo/ sound spelled **ew**.

7.–15. Write the words that have the /oo/ sound spelled **oo**.

REMEMBER THE SPELLING STRATEGY

Remember that the /oo/ sound can be spelled in different ways: **oo** in **pool** and **ew** in **chew**.

Spelling ^{and} Phonics

Sounds and Letters

1.–5. Write the spelling words that end with the /oo͞/ sound. Circle the word that begins with a silent consonant.

6.–8. Write **pool** and the spelling words that rhyme with **pool**. Circle the letters that spell the /oo͞/ sound.

Word Structure

9. Replace the first letter in **moose** to make a spelling word.

10. Replace the last letter in **root** to make this spelling word.

11. Replace one letter in **short** to make a spelling word.

12. Add one letter to the word **chose** to make a spelling word.

USING THE Dictionary

A dictionary has three parts.

Front a–g	Middle h–p	Back q–z
smooth	news	balloon

13. Which word in the box is found in the front?

14. Which word in the box is found in the back?

15. Which word in the box is found in the middle?

Spelling and Reading

crew	loose	news	school	drew
knew	smooth	pool	shoot	threw
roof	fool	chew	balloon	choose

Solve the Analogies Write a spelling word to complete each analogy.

1. **Dull** is to **sharp** as **rough** is to _____.
2. **Touch** is to **feel** as **pick** is to _____.
3. **Eyes** are to **see** as **teeth** are to _____.
4. **Sleep** is to **bed** as **swim** is to _____.
5. **Thick** is to **thin** as **tight** is to _____.
6. **Box** is to **lid** as **house** is to _____.
7. **Joke** is to **cheer** as **trick** is to _____.

Complete the Sentences Write a spelling word from the box to complete each sentence.

balloon	news	school	crew
shoot	knew	drew	threw

8. Marcy went to _____ on Monday.
9. John Glenn was part of the space shuttle's _____.
10. We heard important _____.
11. The scientists will _____ a rocket into space.
12. Our class _____ pictures of a space capsule.
13. Did the hot air _____ drift above the trees?
14. Martin _____ the ball through the hoop.
15. Mr. Debbs's class _____ about the test.

34

Spelling and Writing

Proofread a News Story

Five words are not spelled correctly in this news story. Write the words correctly.

In our schol, we get a balloon every time we read a book. One day, we put air into all the balloons. Then we let them lose to fly away over the roff. The sky was filled with colors. Then we wrote nooz stories and droow pictures.

Proofreading Marks

≡   Make a capital.

/   Make a small letter.

∧   Add something.

ℓ   Take out something.

⊙   Add a period.

New paragraph

SP   Spelling error

Write a News Story

Narrative Writing

Write a news story about something special that happened at your school. Include information about

- what happened.
- where it happened.
- when it happened.
- how it happened.
- why it happened.

Use as many spelling words as you can.

Write a title that tells what your story is about.

Writing Process

Prewriting

⇩

Drafting

⇩

Revising

⇩

Editing

⇩

Publishing

Proofread Your Writing During ▶

Proofread your writing for spelling errors as part of the editing stage in the writing process. Be sure to check each word carefully. Use a dictionary to check spelling if you are not sure.

VOCABULARY CONNECTIONS

►Strategy Words◄

Review Words: ew, oo

Write a word from the box that rhymes with the underlined word.

blew	boot	grew	noon

1. I lost my <u>suit</u>, but I found my _____.
2. The light of the <u>moon</u> cannot be seen at _____.
3. It started out with a <u>few</u>, but then the crowd _____.
4. The leaves <u>flew</u> as the wind _____.

Preview Words: ew, oo

Write the word from the box that matches each clue.

dew	loop	review	toot

5. To tie your shoes, you need to make one of these.
6. Before you take a test, it is best to do this.
7. This can sometimes be found early in the morning on grass.
8. A car does this with a horn.

Content Words

Science: Plants

Write the word from the box that fits each definition.

greenhouse	roots	seedling	bloom

1. A young plant grown from a seed is a _____.
2. The parts of the plant that are usually underground are its _____.
3. The flower of a plant is also called a _____.
4. A house built mostly of glass to control the temperature and help plants grow is a _____.

Math: Relationships

Write the word that belongs in each blank.

numbers	less	equal	greater

5. Five is _____ than four.
6. We count using _____.
7. Four is _____ than seven.
8. The sides of a square are _____.

Apply the Spelling Strategy

Circle the letters that spell the /o͞o/ sound in two of the Content Words you wrote.

Word Study

Compound Words

A **compound word** is made of two or more smaller words. **Beeswax** is a compound word. Write the Content Word that is a compound word.

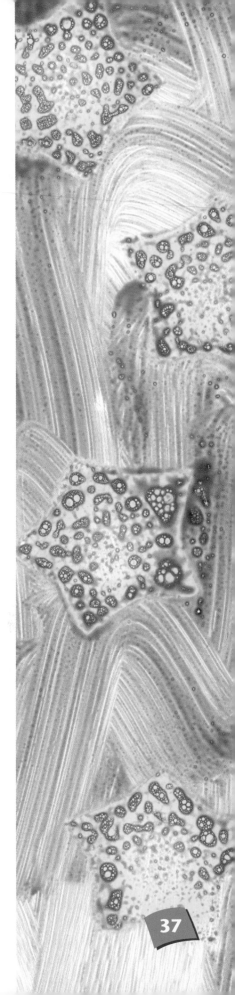

37

Assessment Units 1–5

Each Assessment Word in the box fits one of the spelling strategies you have studied over the past five weeks. Read the spelling strategies. Then write each Assessment Word under the unit number it fits.

Unit 1 _____

1.–3. The **short a** sound you hear in **plan** is spelled **a**. The **short i** sound you hear in **trip** is spelled **i**.

Unit 2 _____

4.–6. The **short o** sound you hear in **drop** is spelled **o**. The **short e** sound you hear in **desk** is spelled **e**.

Unit 3 _____

7.–9. The **short u** sound can be spelled in different ways: **u** in **lunch** and **o** in **become**.

Unit 4 _____

10.–12. The **/oi/** sound you hear in **oil** is spelled **oi**. The **/ou/** sound you hear in **loud** is spelled **ou**.

Unit 5 _____

13.–15. The **/oo/** sound can be spelled in different ways: **oo** in **pool** and **ew** in **chew**.

fund

stout

groom

damp

troop

son

hound

track

ton

coop

bent

shock

toil

lend

trim

plan	stick	grand	stamp	list	act	trip

Write the spelling word that goes with each clue.

1. Add **l** to **pan**.
2. Add **t** to **sick**.
3. Add **r** to **tip**.
4. Change **e** to **t** in **ace**.
5. Change **nd** to **mp** in **stand**.
6. Change **n** to **s** in **lint**.
7. Change **st** to **gr** in **stand**.

Review Unit 2: Short o, Short e

drop	spend	clock	spent	nest	desk	block

Write a spelling word for each clue.

8. You have one. Your teacher has one. You may be seated at it right now.
9. It might be made of wood. It has several sides. You can stack one on top of another.
10. It has hands, but never washes them. There is probably one in your room.
11. It is made of twigs, but birds call it home.

Write a spelling word to complete each sentence.

12. By Thursday, Jake had _____ his week's allowance.
13. If I save my money, I will have $2.00 to _____.
14. Be careful not to _____ the glasses.

39

Review — Unit 3: Short u

| none | until | love | nothing | study | buzz | under |

Write the spelling word for each clue.

1. This word rhymes with **dove**.
2. This word rhymes with **does**.
3. This word rhymes with **thunder**.
4. This word rhymes with **sun**.
5. This word ends in **ing**.
6. This word rhymes with **muddy**.
7. This word means "up to the time."

Review — Unit 4: ou, oi

| point | house | voice | ground | south | loud | join |

Write a spelling word to complete each sentence. The word you write will rhyme with the underlined word.

8. The <u>crowd</u> at the game gave a _____ cheer for their team.

9. "Please make your <u>choice</u>," said the clerk with a kind _____.

10. Flip a <u>coin</u> to decide which team you will _____.

11. The doctor asked me to _____ to the <u>joint</u> that hurt.

12. Can I go _____ to reach the <u>mouth</u> of the river?

13. We found a <u>mouse</u> had made its _____ in the woodpile.

14. I <u>found</u> my book lying on the _____.

Review Unit 5: ew, oo

| threw | school | knew | choose | balloon | roof | news |

Write the spelling word that completes each sentence.

1. Throw the ball the way I _____ it to you.
2. I know you thought I _____ what to do.
3. That story is really old _____.
4. The string on my yellow _____ broke.
5. It floated high up over the _____ of the house.
6. Everyone in my class at _____ saw it go.
7. You may _____ any color you like.

GAME **Spelling Study Strategy**

Circle Dot

One good way to practice spelling words is to make it into a game. Play **Circle Dot** to practice your spelling.

Find a partner. Each partner should write a list of 15 spelling words. Trade lists and read your lists aloud. Help each other read and pronounce the words.

Then your partner should read one word from your list aloud. You write that word on a piece of paper. When you finish, your partner should spell the word out loud, one letter at a time.

As your partner says each letter, make a dot under each correct letter on your page. If you have a letter that is not correct, draw a circle under the letter. If you have left out a letter, make a little circle to show where it should have been. The circles will show where you have trouble. Write the word again and check the spelling.

Take turns as you play **Circle Dot**.

Grammar, Usage, and Mechanics

Kinds of Sentences

There are four kinds of sentences. Each ends with a special mark.

Telling Sentence:	My friend will come, too.
Asking Sentence:	Have you met her?
Command:	Move over, please.
Sentence That Shows Strong Feeling:	This is fun!

Practice Activity

A. What kind of sentence is each one? Write **telling** or **asking** to answer the question.

1. My bus is yellow.
2. Is that your sister?
3. Are you in my class?
4. We can walk home.
5. Our team won the game.

B. What kind of sentence is each one? Write **command** or **feeling** to answer the question.

6. What a funny joke!
7. Wait at the corner.
8. Call your father at work.
9. This juice is great!
10. Bring me the paper, please.

WORKSHOP

Proofreading Strategy

Circle and Check

Good writers always proofread their writing for spelling errors. Here's a strategy you can use to proofread your papers.

Instead of reading your paper the regular way, look at just the first word. Is it spelled right? If you know that it is, go on and read the next word. If you are not sure of the spelling, circle the word and then go on to the next. Look at each word in your paper this way.

Electronic Spelling

File Names

Writing with a word processor is fun. You do not have to recopy everything. You can also put in pictures, charts, and fancy headlines. You can create many works that you want to save.

When you save work on a computer, you save it in a file. You must give this file a name. If you misspell the file name, you may not be able to find it later.

Which of these file names has spelling mistakes in them? Write those words correctly. Write **OK** if a name is correct.

1. studey page
2. schole work
3. the latest news
4. plon for the day
5. word list
6. money spint

Spelling and Thinking

READ THE SPELLING WORDS

1. state	*state*	In which **state** do you live?
2. close	*close*	Please **close** the door as you leave.
3. slide	*slide*	The boy went down the water **slide**.
4. face	*face*	Tanja drew a happy **face**.
5. globe	*globe*	A **globe** is a round map of the world.
6. pave	*pave*	The workers will **pave** the street.
7. size	*size*	Mary's shoes are the wrong **size**.
8. smoke	*smoke*	My eyes tear when I smell **smoke**.
9. flame	*flame*	The **flame** set the grease on fire.
10. broke	*broke*	The glass **broke** into pieces.
11. prize	*prize*	Carla won first **prize** at the fair.
12. skate	*skate*	Juanita learned to **skate** on ice.
13. smile	*smile*	A baby will **smile** when it is happy.
14. plane	*plane*	David went to New York by **plane**.
15. stone	*stone*	The **stone** in her shoe hurt her toe.

SORT THE SPELLING WORDS

Write the words that have

1.–6. the **long a** sound spelled **vowel-consonant-e**.

7.–10. the **long i** sound spelled **vowel-consonant-e**.

11.–15. the **long o** sound spelled **vowel-consonant-e**.

REMEMBER THE SPELLING STRATEGY

Remember that the long vowel sounds you hear in **pave,** **size,** and **globe** are spelled **vowel-consonant-e.**

44

Beginning Sounds

1.–6. Write the spelling words that begin with an **s** and another consonant. Draw a line under the first two consonants.

7.–8. Write the spelling words that begin with a **p** and another consonant. Draw a line under the first two consonants.

Rhyming Words

9. Write a spelling word that rhymes with **lace**.

10. Write a spelling word that rhymes with **blame**.

11. Write a spelling word that rhymes with **cave**.

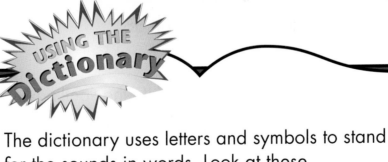

USING THE Dictionary

The dictionary uses letters and symbols to stand for the sounds in words. Look at these dictionary letters and symbols. Say each word, then write the spelling word. Use the pronunciation key in your **Spelling Dictionary**.

12. /brōk/

13. /sīz/

14. /glōb/

15. /klōz/

Spelling and Reading

state	close	slide	face	globe
pave	size	smoke	flame	broke
prize	skate	smile	plane	stone

Solve the Analogies Write a spelling word to complete each analogy.

1. **Bottle** is to **cap** as **door** is to _____.
2. **Toes** are to **foot** as **nose** is to _____.
3. **Square** is to **cube** as **round** is to _____.
4. **Water** is to **swim** as **ice** is to _____.
5. **Land** is to **car** as **air** is to _____.
6. **Cold** is to **ice** as **hot** is to _____.

Use the Clues Write the spelling word for each clue.

7. I rise through a chimney.
8. I can also be called a rock.
9. I am given as a reward.
10. I am something your face can do.
11. I am often found on a playground.

Complete the Paragraph Write the spelling words from the box that complete the paragraph.

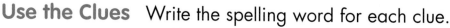

state	broke	pave	size

Workers came to the road to fill and __12.__ a hole. The __13.__ of the hole was large. Heavy trucks used the road so much that the surface __14.__ up. The government of our __15.__ pays for road repair.

Spelling and Writing

Proofread Interview Questions

Five words are not spelled correctly in these interview questions. Write the words correctly.

1. How did you learn to skate so well?
2. Did you slyde often when you practiced?
3. Did you hit a stone when you broak your leg?
4. Did you ever fall on your fase?
5. How did you feel when you lost the prise at the stat meet?

Write Interview Questions

Pretend you are going to interview a sports figure. Write some questions you would like to ask, such as

- how the person became interested in the sport.
- why the person likes the sport.
- what special prizes the person has received.

Be sure to leave some space after each question for the answer. Use as many spelling words as you can.

Proofread Your Writing During Editing

Proofread your writing for spelling errors. Be sure to check each word carefully. Use a dictionary to check spelling if you are not sure.

Writing Process

Prewriting

⇩

Drafting

⇩

Revising

⇩

Editing

⇩

Publishing

47

Unit 7 enrichment

VOCABULARY CONNECTIONS

Strategy Words

Review Words: Vowel-Consonant-e

Write the word from the box that matches each clue.

cake	dime	joke	mule

1. I have candles on me for your birthday.
2. I look like a horse with long ears.
3. I am a silvery coin.
4. People laugh when you tell this.

Preview Words: Vowel-Consonant-e

Write the word from the box that completes each sentence.

alive	scene	scrape	tube

5. Is there any glue left in this _____?
6. The kitten that got lost is _____ and well.
7. Please _____ the ice off the window so I can see.
8. My class will perform the first _____ of the play at noon.

48

Content Words

Fine Arts: Drawing

Write the word that completes the meaning.

sketch	scribble	doodle	trace

Miss Stall gave Tim some thin paper and asked him to __1.__ a copy of a picture in a book. Tim drew a rough __2.__ of it instead. He also decided to __3.__ notes to himself about the picture. Finally, he decided just to __4.__ on some scrap paper.

Science: Respiratory System

Write the word from the box that matches each clue.

heart	living	beat	breath

5. A plant or animal that is not dead is this.
6. This is an organ in your body that pumps blood.
7. This means "to pound again and again."
8. This can be seen in cold weather.

Apply the Spelling Strategy

Circle the letters that spell the **long a** vowel sound in one of the Content Words you wrote.

Word Study

Word History

Scribere is an old word that meant "to write." Write the Content Word that comes from this word. It means "a quick way of writing."

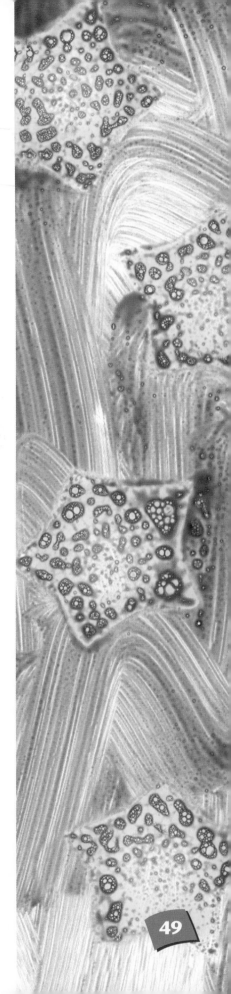

49

Spelling ^a_n_d Thinking

READ THE SPELLING WORDS

1. aid	*aid*	A map is a useful **aid** on a trip.
2. pay	*pay*	How much did you **pay** for the pen?
3. chain	*chain*	Tina wears a golden **chain**.
4. mail	*mail*	Did you **mail** my letter?
5. tray	*tray*	Put the glasses on the **tray**.
6. paint	*paint*	We will **paint** my room yellow.
7. maybe	*maybe*	If we try, **maybe** we will win.
8. plain	*plain*	I like to wear **plain** shirts.
9. lay	*lay*	Please **lay** my crayons down.
10. main	*main*	We went to the **main** building.
11. always	*always*	Is he **always** late?
12. pail	*pail*	Another word for **pail** is bucket.
13. laid	*laid*	The hen **laid** an egg.
14. away	*away*	Please throw **away** the empty box.
15. paid	*paid*	Did you get **paid** for the work?

SORT THE SPELLING WORDS

1.–9. Write the words in which the **long a** sound is spelled **ai**.

10.–15. Write the words in which the **long a** sound is spelled **ay**.

REMEMBER THE SPELLING STRATEGY

Remember that the **long a** sound can be spelled in different ways: **ai** in **paint** and **ay** in **tray**.

Ending Sounds

I.–3. Write **aid** and the spelling words that rhyme with **aid**.

4.–5. Write **mail** and the spelling word that rhymes with **mail**.

6.–8. Write **main** and the spelling words that rhyme with **main**.

Word Structure

9. Add the letter **a** to **way** to make this spelling word.

10. Add the letters **be** to **may** to make this spelling word.

11. Add the letters **al** to **ways** to make this spelling word.

12. Drop one letter from **play** to make this spelling word.

USING THE Dictionary

To find a word that has an ending added, you must look up the base word. Write the word you would look up to find the meaning of each of these words.

13. trays   **14.** paying   **15.** painted

◆ ◆ ◆

Dictionary Check Be sure to check the base words in your **Spelling Dictionary**.

Spelling ᴬⁿᵈ Reading

aid	pay	chain	mail	tray
paint	maybe	plain	lay	main
always	pail	laid	away	paid

Word Groups Read each set of words. Add the spelling word that belongs in each group.

1. tub, bucket, _____
2. never, sometimes, _____
3. common, simple, _____
4. crayon, marker, _____
5. plate, platter, _____
6. letters, packages, _____
7. probably, perhaps, _____

Complete the Sentences Write the spelling word from the box that completes each sentence.

pay	lay	laid	away	chain	paid	aid	main

8. Will you help me put _____ these games?
9. Please _____ the blanket on the bed.
10. I will come as soon as I _____ for my paper and brushes.
11. Tom has already _____ for his supplies.
12. Someone _____ a book on my chair.
13. Our projects will be shown in the _____ hallway.
14. My mobile is the one hanging from a _____.
15. Glasses may _____ your sight.

Spelling and Writing

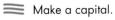
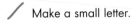

Proofread a Paragraph

Five words are not spelled correctly in this paragraph. Write the words correctly.

> # Buy by Catalog!
>
> You can send awway for many items by mael. You might want to order some paynt or a gold chayne or a useful traye. When it comes time to pay, the company will send you a bill.
>
> | Item | Quantity | Description | | |
> |------|----------|-------------|---|---|
> | | | | | |
> | | | | Total | |

Proofreading Marks

≡	Make a capital.
/	Make a small letter.
∧	Add something.
ℓ	Take out something.
⊙	Add a period.
⌗	New paragraph
SP	Spelling error

Write a Paragraph

Descriptive Writing

Write a paragraph about something you sent away for or would like to send away for. It might be something to wear that you saw in a catalog or a tape advertised on TV.

- Name the item.
- Describe the color, size, or style.
- Tell the price.
- Tell your reader why you want that item.

Use as many spelling words as you can.

Proofread Your Writing During ▶ Editing

Writing Process

Prewriting
⇩
Drafting
⇩
Revising
⇩
Editing
⇩
Publishing

Proofread your writing for spelling errors as part of the editing stage in the writing process. Be sure to check each word carefully. Use a dictionary to check spelling if you are not sure.

Unit 8 enrichment

VOCABULARY CONNECTIONS

◄ Strategy Words ►

Review Words: Long a Spelled ai, ay

Write a word from the box to complete each sentence.

braid	play	spray	train

1. The _____ from the garden hose soaked my new clothes.

2. The _____ pulled slowly into the station.

3. Terry is wearing her hair in a _____.

4. Everyone in my class likes to _____ soccer and basketball.

Preview Words: Long a Spelled ai, ay

Write a word from the box that matches each clue.

holiday	railway	remain	waist

5. This is the part of the body around which a belt is worn.

6. This is another word for **stay**.

7. This is another word for **railroad**.

8. This is a day when people celebrate something special.

54

Content Words

Science: Water

Write a word from the box that matches each clue.

bay	ocean	gulf	beach

1. This is a huge body of salt water.
2. This is the sandy shore of a body of water.
3. This body of water rhymes with the word **way**.
4. This body of water is partly closed in by land. It is usually larger than a bay.

Social Studies: Government

Write the word that completes each sentence.

cities	towns	duty	worker

5. Someone who does a job is known as a _____.
6. Places with many buildings and people are _____.
7. All citizens should do their _____ and vote.
8. Places that are smaller than cities are _____.

Apply the Spelling Strategy

Circle the letters that spell the **long a** sound in one of the Content Words you wrote.

Word Study

Homophones

Words that sound alike but have different spellings and meanings are **homophones**. **Won** and **one** are homophones. Write the Strategy Word that is a homophone for **waste**.

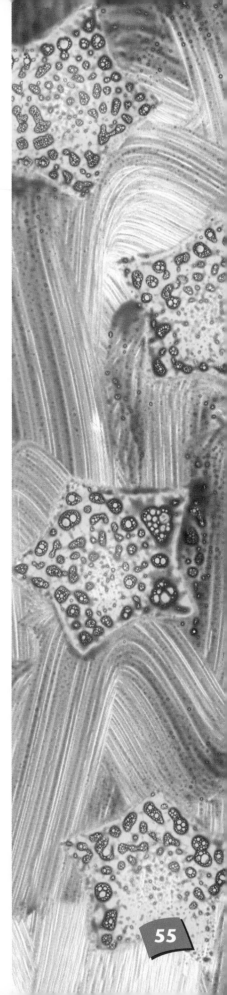

Spelling and Thinking

1. sheep	*sheep*	Farmers keep **sheep** for their wool.
2. dream	*dream*	All people **dream** during sleep.
3. street	*street*	The **street** has much traffic.
4. east	*east*	The sun rises in the **east**.
5. treat	*treat*	Do you **treat** your pet dog well?
6. mean	*mean*	Scaring the child was a **mean** trick.
7. wheels	*wheels*	Bicycle **wheels** vary in size.
8. peace	*peace*	The treaty brought **peace** to the land.
9. real	*real*	The book is about a **real** event.
10. cheese	*cheese*	Milk is used to make **cheese**.
11. leave	*leave*	Sometimes I **leave** early for school.
12. stream	*stream*	A river is a large **stream**.
13. sweet	*sweet*	This candy tastes **sweet**.
14. teacher	*teacher*	My **teacher** helps me learn.
15. heat	*heat*	Fire creates **heat**.

SORT THE SPELLING WORDS

1.–5. Write the spelling words that have the **long e** sound spelled **ee**.

6.–15. Write the spelling words that have the **long e** sound spelled **ea**.

REMEMBER THE SPELLING STRATEGY

Remember that the **long e** sound can be spelled in different ways: **ea** in **treat** and **ee** in **street**.

Sound Patterns

1.–6. Write the spelling words that begin with one consonant. Circle the letters that spell the **long e** sound.

Letter Patterns

Write spelling words by adding the missing letters.

7. st___eam

8. stre___t

9. e___st

10. trea___

Beginnings and Endings

Match the beginnings of the spelling words in the first column with their endings in the second column. Write the spelling words.

11. wh   eam

12. sw   eels

13. dr   eet

USING THE Dictionary

One word in each sentence is the dictionary respelling for a spelling word. Write the spelling word.

14. Warm blankets are made from the wool of /shēp/.

15. Milk is added to make /chēz/.

Spelling and Reading

sheep	dream	street	east	treat
mean	wheels	peace	real	cheese
leave	stream	sweet	teacher	heat

Complete the Sentences Read each sentence below. Write the spelling word that completes each sentence.

1. On cold days I turn on the _____ when I get home.

2. I like to eat crackers with _____.

3. My _____ explained the problem to us.

Answer the Questions Write a spelling word to answer each question.

4. What word names a farm animal?

5. What is the opposite of **imaginary**?

6. What parts of a bicycle are round?

7. What do we do while we are asleep?

8. What is the opposite of **west**?

9. What is the opposite of **kind**?

Complete the Story Write the spelling words from the box that best complete the story.

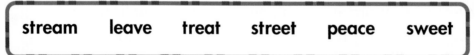

stream	leave	treat	street	peace	sweet

    I like to get lots of exercise and eat healthy foods. When I __10.__ school at the end of the day, I carefully cross the busy __11.__. I enjoy the __12.__ and quiet of the __13.__ that flows near my house. When I get home, my favorite __14.__ is a piece of __15.__ fruit.

Ending Sounds

1. Write the spelling word that rhymes with **wild**. Circle the two consonants at the end of the word.

2. Write the spelling word that rhymes with **sigh**. Circle the silent consonants.

Sound and Letter Patterns

3. Write the spelling word that begins with a silent consonant. Circle the silent consonant.

4. Write the spelling word that begins with a consonant cluster and ends with **t**.

5.–9. Write **night**. Change the first letter to write four more spelling words.

10.–12. Write the spelling words that end with **nd**. Circle the letters that spell the **long i** sound.

USING THE Dictionary

Find **sigh, sign,** and **wild** in your **Spelling Dictionary**. Write the spelling word that goes with each meaning.

13. not tamed; not cultivated; living or growing in a natural condition

14. a long, deep breathing sound

15. a notice or board with writing on it

night	bright	find	light	wild
high	blind	fight	sight	kind
sign	knight	mild	right	sigh

Find the Opposites Write the spelling word that is the opposite in meaning of each of these words.

1. low
2. left
3. day
4. seeing clearly
5. heavy

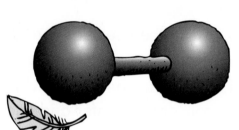

Complete the Meanings Write the spelling word that belongs in each sentence.

6. The directions on the road _____ helped us find our way.
7. The army had to _____ for freedom.
8. What _____ of story do you like to read?
9. The museum has a suit of armor worn by a _____.
10. The forests were a beautiful _____.
11. Do you like your chili hot or _____?

Complete the Story Write the spelling words from the box that best complete the story.

sigh	wild	bright	find

Jamaal was exploring a __12.__, sunny field. He hoped to __13.__ butterflies. Instead, he saw a raccoon. He gave a __14.__ of relief when the __15.__ animal ran the other way.

Spelling and Writing

Proofread a Paragraph

Five words are not spelled correctly in this paragraph. Write the words correctly.

Our country is a land of many amazing sights. Some are natural wonders. Many people fynd the Grand Canyon and Yellowstone National Park beautiful with their wonderful landscapes and wilde rivers. Others like the highe Rocky Mountains. Still others like the underground Carlsbad Caverns, where it is always nite, except when there is brite light.

Proofreading Marks

≡ Make a capital.

/ Make a small letter.

∧ Add something.

℮ Take out something.

⊙ Add a period.

⌗ New paragraph

ⓈⓅ Spelling error

Write a Paragraph

Narrative Writing

A topic sentence gives the main idea of a paragraph. Detail sentences give specific facts about the main idea. Choose one of the following topic sentences or write your own. Then write detail sentences to make a paragraph.

- A day in the life of a student is very busy.
- A funny thing happened to me yesterday.
- Collecting baseball cards is a good hobby.

Use as many spelling words as you can.

Proofread Your Writing During ▶

Writing Process

Prewriting
⇩
Drafting
⇩
Revising
⇩
Editing
⇩
Publishing

Proofread your writing for spelling errors as part of the editing stage in the writing process. Be sure to check each word carefully. Use a dictionary to check the spelling if you are not sure.

◄Strategy Words►

Review Words: Long i Spelled i, igh

Write the word from the box that matches each clue.

ivory	lion	shiny	tiger

1. A male one of these has a mane.
2. A very large wild cat that has black stripes is known by this name.
3. A new penny is said to be this.
4. This is another name for an elephant's tusks.

Preview Words: Long i Spelled i, igh

Write the word from the box to complete each sentence.

libraries	might	slight	title

5. The name of an article or a book is its _____.
6. You can borrow books and many other items from _____.
7. We _____ go to the zoo tomorrow.
8. There is a _____ error in that sentence.

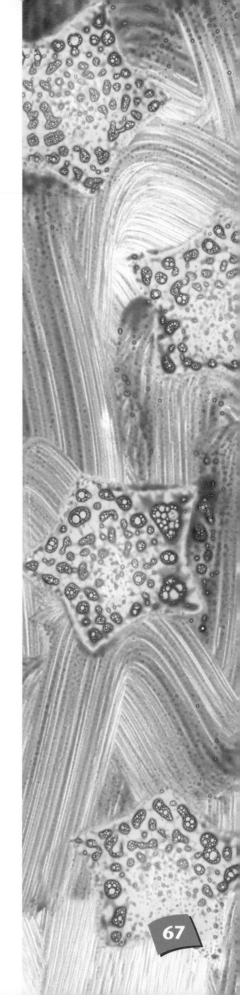

Content Words

Math: Operations

Write a word from the box that matches each clue.

math	multiply	subtract	divide

1. the opposite of **divide**
2. the opposite of **add**
3. the opposite of **multiply**
4. a shortened form of the word **mathematics**

Social Studies: Careers

Write the word from the box that names the worker you might find in each of these places.

pilot	driver	firefighter	clerk

5. at an airport
6. at a shopping center
7. in a bus
8. at a burning building

Apply the Spelling Strategy

Circle the letters that spell the **long i** sound **i** or **igh** in two of the Content Words you wrote.

Word Study

Coined Words

A **coined word** is made up to name something new. **Liger** is a coined word. It names an animal whose parents are two different kinds of big cats. One parent is a lion. Can you guess what animal the other parent is? Write the Strategy Word that names it.

67

Spelling and Thinking

READ THE SPELLING WORDS

1. snow — *snow* — The new **snow** is white and fresh.
2. load — *load* — The mule has a heavy **load** on its back.
3. almost — *almost* — I am **almost** nine years old.
4. row — *row* — We **row** the boat across the lake.
5. soak — *soak* — I **soak** my sore foot in hot water.
6. window — *window* — The **window** lets in a lot of light.
7. foam — *foam* — Wind makes **foam** appear on the water.
8. most — *most* — I am friends with **most** of the girls.
9. flow — *flow* — Does this river **flow** into the ocean?
10. goat — *goat* — We get milk and cheese from a **goat**.
11. throw — *throw* — Please **throw** me the ball.
12. float — *float* — I can **float** on the water.
13. blow — *blow* — The guards will **blow** their trumpets.
14. below — *below* — Your coat is **below** mine in the pile.
15. soap — *soap* — Wash with warm water and **soap**.

SORT THE SPELLING WORDS

1.–7. Write the words with the **long o** sound spelled **ow**.

8.–13. Write the words with the **long o** sound spelled **oa**.

14.–15. Write the words with the **long o** sound spelled **o**.

REMEMBER THE SPELLING STRATEGY

Remember that the **long o** sound can be spelled: **ow** in **blow, oa** in **float,** and **o** in **most.**

68

Spelling and Phonics

Rhyming Groups

Write the spelling word that belongs in each rhyming group.

1. toad, road, _____
2. home, roam, _____
3. hope, rope, _____
4. joke, woke, _____

Word Structure

Replace the underlined letters in each word to make a spelling word.

5. r<u>ed</u>
6. fl<u>oor</u>
7. fla<u>g</u>
8. g<u>oo</u>d

9. thr<u>ee</u>
10. bl<u>ue</u>
11. sna<u>p</u>
12. mor<u>e</u>

USING THE Dictionary

Your dictionary shows a • between syllables of entry words. Write these words with a • between the syllables.

13. almost   14. below   15. window

◆ ◆ ◆

Dictionary Check Be sure to check the syllables in your **Spelling Dictionary**.

Spelling and Reading

snow	load	almost	row	soak
window	foam	most	flow	goat
throw	float	blow	below	soap

Replace the Words Write the spelling word that could best replace the underlined word or words.

1. We are <u>just about</u> ready to start studying for the spelling bee.

2. Please put these desks in a <u>straight line</u>.

3. We stood on the bridge and looked at the river <u>under</u> us.

4. Tim will <u>pitch</u> the trash into the can.

5. Maria helped us <u>pile</u> the wood into the back of the large truck.

6. The sink was filled with <u>bubbles</u>.

Complete the Sentences Write a spelling word to complete each sentence.

7. That shirt will come clean if we _____ it overnight.

8. Use a lot of _____ on your dirty hands.

9. Do you think our raft will _____?

10. The wind began to _____ hard as the hurricane got closer to the coast.

11. A _____ has horns and hooves.

12. This stream will _____ into the river.

13. This _____ will melt soon.

14. Which class in your school has the _____ students in it?

15. The baseball went through the _____ and shattered the glass.

Spelling and Writing

Proofread Directions

Five words are not spelled correctly in this set of directions. Write the words correctly.

Jumping in a wave is fun. To have the moast fun, do it right. Wait until the wave is almost ready to crash. Then dive into it. To do this, thro yourself into the wave just belo its top. Keep your mouth shut and bloe air out through your nose. Then just flote!

Proofreading Marks

≡ Make a capital.

／ Make a small letter.

∧ Add something.

ℓ Take out something.

⊙ Add a period.

New paragraph

SP Spelling error

Write Directions

Expository Writing

Think of something you like to do or know how to do well. There are many things you do well, but choose just one. That might be delivering newspapers, making a sandwich, brushing your teeth, or grooming a horse. Before writing your draft take the following steps.

- Tell all the steps to take.
- Write the steps in the correct order.

Use as many spelling words as you can.

Writing Process

Prewriting

⇩

Drafting

⇩

Revising

⇩

Proofread Your Writing During   **Editing**

⇩

Publishing

Proofread your writing for spelling errors as part of the editing stage in the writing process. Be sure to check each word carefully. Use a dictionary to check spelling if you are not sure.

71

◄Strategy Words►

Review Words: Long o Spelled ow, oa, o

Write a word from the box for each clue.

coat	follow	grow	road

1. This word has two syllables and a double consonant in its spelling.
2. This word rhymes with **toad**.
3. This word has a /**k**/ sound, but it does not have the letter **k** in its spelling.
4. This word begins with two consonants together and rhymes with **throw**.

Preview Words: Long o Spelled ow, oa, o

Write a word from the box to complete each analogy.

coast	fold	pillow	solo

5. **Table** is to **plate** as **bed** is to _____.
6. **Many** is to **together** as **one** is to _____.
7. **Mix** is to **stir** as **bend** is to _____.
8. **Marsh** is to **swamp** as **shoreline** is to _____.

Content Words

Math: Measurement

Write the word that answers each question.

gallon	pint	pound	measure

1. Which is a unit of weight?
2. Which means "to find the size of something"?
3. Which equals four quarts?
4. Which equals two cups?

Social Studies: Geography

Write the word from the box that fits each meaning.

highland	grassland	desert	lowland

5. an area of land lower than the land around it
6. a dry region, sometimes covered with sand
7. an area of land higher and more hilly than the land around it
8. open land that is covered with grass

Apply the Spelling Strategy

Circle the letters that spell the **long o** sound in one of the Content Words you wrote.

Word Study

Shades of Meaning

When words mean almost but not quite the same thing, we say they have different **shades of meaning**. For example, **munch** and **bite** name different ways to chew. Write the Strategy Word that fits with the meaning of these words: **highway, street, _____.**

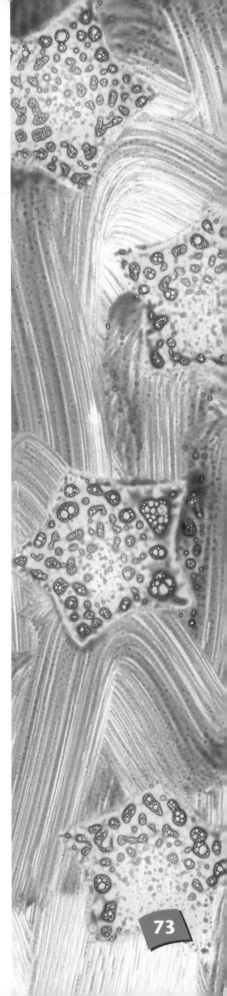

73

Assessment and Review

Assessment Units 7–11

Each Assessment Word in the box fits one of the spelling strategies you have studied over the past five weeks. Read the spelling strategies. Then write each Assessment Word under the unit number it fits.

Unit 7 _____

1.–3. The long vowel sounds you hear in **pave, size,** and **globe** are spelled **vowel-consonant-e.**

Unit 8 _____

4.–6. The **long a** sound can be spelled in different ways: **ai** in **paint** and **ay** in **tray.**

Unit 9 _____

7.–9. The **long e** sound can be spelled in different ways: **ea** in **treat** and **ee** in **street.**

Unit 10 _____

10.–12. The **long i** sound can be spelled in different ways: **i** in **kind** and **igh** in **sigh.**

Unit 11 _____

13.–15. The **long o** sound can be spelled: **ow** in **blow, oa** in **float,** and **o** in **most.**

| stripe |
| bail |
| cream |
| bind |
| groan |
| sold |
| thigh |
| bead |
| bait |
| brave |
| fellow |
| rind |
| creep |
| sway |
| grove |

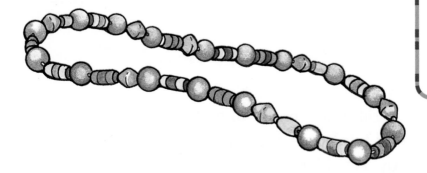

broke	smile	close	state	face	stone	size

Write the spelling words by taking the **-ing** off the words below and adding the final **e**.

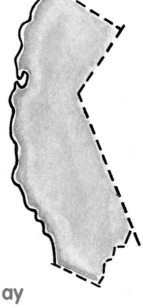

1. smiling
2. closing
3. facing
4. sizing

Write the spelling word that completes the sentence.

5. The plate _____ when I dropped it.
6. The _____ of California is on the west coast of the United States.
7. Another word for **rock** is _____.

Review Unit 8: Long a Spelled ai, ay

always	chain	laid	maybe	mail	pay	main

Write the spelling word that rhymes with each word.

8. day
9. braid
10. baby

Find the word that is misspelled in each sentence. Write the word correctly.

11. I alwaz try to help a friend in trouble.
12. The magazine was delivered with our mayle.
13. The mayn gate of the garden was locked.
14. The swing fell when the chian broke.

 Unit 9: Long e Spelled ee, ea

| real | teacher | street | wheels | east | heat | stream |

Write the spelling word that completes the sentence.

1. The sun comes up in the _____.
2. I could see many fish in the clear _____.
3. That moving truck has many _____.
4. In front of my school is a wide _____.
5. The fruit in that picture looks almost _____.
6. The reading _____ gave them each a book.
7. The fire gave out a lot of _____.

 **Review** Unit 10: Long i Spelled i, igh

| bright | mild | kind | right | night | sign | high |

Write the spelling word that completes the sentence.

8. My uncle likes his chili hot and spicy instead of _____.
9. There is a "For Sale" _____ in front of that house.
10. I am not afraid to jump off the _____ diving board.

Write the spelling word that means the opposite of the underlined word in these sentences.

11. The clerk had a <u>mean</u> look on her face.
12. This is the <u>day</u> I have been waiting for.
13. Warren got every question on the test <u>wrong</u>.
14. The <u>dim</u> light of the moon lighted the path.

| almost | snow | float | window | below | goat | soap |

Write the spelling word that means about the same as the word or words below.

1. to drift on water   2. under   3. nearly

Write the spelling word that completes the sentence.

4. The cold rain will soon turn to _____.

5. Farmer Olson kept a prize _____ at his farm.

6. Be careful not to slip on the _____ in the shower.

7. Open the _____ to let in some fresh air.

Spelling Study Strategy

Sorting by Vowel Spelling Patterns

Write spelling words on small cards. Then sort the words by spelling pattern.

1. Make a stack of words in which ow spells **long o**.

2. Make a stack of words in which ay spells **long a**.

3. Make a stack of words in which ee spells **long e**.

4. Make a stack of words in which igh spells **long i**.

5. Make a stack of words in which ai spells **long a**.

6. Make a stack of words in which ea spells **long e**.

7. Make a stack of words in which **vowel-consonant-e** spells **long o**.

8. Read your words to a partner. Then read your partner's list.

Unit 12 enrichment

Grammar, Usage, and Mechanics

Singular and Plural Nouns

A singular noun names one person, place, or thing.

    The **girl** has a **cat**.

    The **boat** has a **sail**.

A plural noun names more than one person, place, or thing.

    The **girls** own many **cats**.

    These **boats** have many **sails**.

Many plural nouns are formed by adding an **-s** to the end of the singular noun.

Practice Activity

A. Write the singular noun used to make each plural below.

    1. teachers   3. nights   5. streets

    2. stones   4. windows   6. prizes

B. Each sentence has one plural noun. Write the plural nouns.

    7. My dog has blue eyes.

    8. The students left the classroom.

    9. Dry your hands with this towel.

    10. Look at the flowers on that tree!

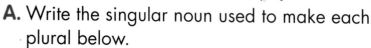

WORKSHOP

Box It!

Good writers always proofread their writing for spelling errors. Here's a strategy that you can use to proofread your work.

Use your fingers to box in each word in your writing. Put your left pointer finger before each word, and put your right pointer finger after it. That way, you are not looking at a sentence but only at a word. Check the spelling of that word and then box in the next word. Continue in this way until you are done.

When you box in words this way, you pay attention to each word instead of to the sentences. You are then more likely to see spelling mistakes. Try it!

Electronic Spelling

Compound Computer Words

Computers have changed the world. They have also changed the way we write. People now use words that did not exist fifty years ago. They also use old words in new ways. Some of these words are so new that spell checkers don't even know them.

Many of these words are compound words—words made by putting smaller words together. For example, **layout** is a compound word. To spell a compound, spell each small word inside it: **lay** and **out**. Now you are the spell checker!

Each compound word below has one of its smaller words misspelled. Write the compound word correctly.

1. uppload
2. keywerd
3. boockmark
4. checkboks
5. settup
6. tulbar

79

Spelling and Thinking

READ THE SPELLING WORDS

1.	shape	*shape*	A square is a **shape** with four sides.
2.	church	*church*	Many people go to a **church** or temple.
3.	watch	*watch*	Let's **watch** the game on television.
4.	father	*father*	My **father** taught me to throw a ball.
5.	wrap	*wrap*	We **wrap** the gifts in pretty paper.
6.	check	*check*	Put a **check** mark next to each word.
7.	finish	*finish*	I will **finish** the book tonight.
8.	sharp	*sharp*	That knife has a very **sharp** edge.
9.	mother	*mother*	My **mother** showed me how to bat.
10.	write	*write*	I will **write** an e-mail message to you.
11.	catch	*catch*	Throw the ball, and I will **catch** it.
12.	chase	*chase*	Do not let the dog **chase** the cat.
13.	shall	*shall*	I **shall** call you in the morning.
14.	thick	*thick*	This **thick** coat will keep you warm.
15.	wrote	*wrote*	Nan **wrote** me a letter yesterday.

SORT THE SPELLING WORDS

1.–4. Write the words that end with **ck** or **tch**.

5.–15. Write the words that are spelled with **wr, ch, sh,** or **th**.

REMEMBER THE SPELLING STRATEGY

Remember that two consonants together can spell a single sound: **wr** in **wrap** and **ck** in **thick**. Two or more consonants can spell new sounds called **consonant digraphs: ch** in **chase, sh** in **shape, th** in **mother,** and **tch** in **watch**.

Spelling ᴬⁿᵈ Phonics

Sound and Letter Patterns

Write the spelling words by adding the missing letters.

1. __ __ ape
2. cat __ __
3. __ __ ote
4. c __ e __ __
5. __ __ i __ k

Word Clues

Write a spelling word for each clue.

6. This word rhymes with **harp**.
7. male parent
8. Change one letter in **shell** to make this word.
9. It rhymes with **face**.
10. female parent
11. You see the word **fin** in this word.
12. It begins and ends with the same two letters.

USING THE Dictionary

The words in a dictionary are in a-b-c order.

13.–15. Write these words in a-b-c order.

wrap   watch   write

◆ ◆ ◆

Dictionary Check Be sure to check the a-b-c order of your words in your **Spelling Dictionary**.

shape	church	watch	father	wrap
check	finish	sharp	mother	write
catch	chase	shall	thick	wrote

Complete the Story   Write the spelling words to complete the story.

"What time __1.__ I meet you on Sunday?" Jenny asked.

Mike said, "I forgot to tell you. My __2.__ and __3.__ will drop me off there after __4.__."

"Great!" said Jenny. "That will give me time to __5.__ my morning chores. I also have to __6.__ my little cousin for a while."

Mike said, "I will be there at 10 o'clock __7.__. I will __8.__ it down so that I don't forget!"

Complete the Rhymes   Write a spelling word that fits each sentence. The spelling word will rhyme with the underlined word.

9. Let Jim read the <u>note</u>. I don't know what she _____.

10. Please check the <u>latch</u>. Did you hear it _____?

11. Look at this <u>grape</u>. It has a funny _____.

12. Which sweater would you <u>pick</u>? I think this one is too _____.

13. Is there a bug on my <u>neck</u>? Would you please _____?

14. I must pick up the <u>pace</u>. I am falling behind in the _____.

15. First, loosen the <u>flap</u>. Then tear off the _____.

Spelling and Writing

Proofread a Poem

Five words are not spelled correctly in this poem. Write the words correctly.

Just Fishing

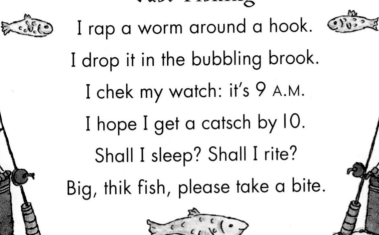

I rap a worm around a hook.

I drop it in the bubbling brook.

I chek my watch: it's 9 A.M.

I hope I get a catsch by 10.

Shall I sleep? Shall I rite?

Big, thik fish, please take a bite.

Write a Poem

Descriptive Writing

Write a poem about a sport or hobby you enjoy. The lines of your poem do not have to rhyme. Be sure to tell

- what you enjoy.
- where, when, or how you do it.
- some details about what you see, do, taste, touch, hear, or smell.

Use as many spelling words as you can.

Writing Process

Prewriting
⇩
Drafting
⇩
Revising
⇩
Editing
⇩
Publishing

Proofread Your Writing During Editing

Proofread your writing for spelling errors as part of the editing stage in the writing process. Be sure to check each word carefully. Use a dictionary to check spelling if you are not sure.

83

Unit 13 enrichment

VOCABULARY CONNECTIONS

Strategy Words

Review Words:
   sh, ch, tch, th, wr, ck

Write a word from the box for each clue.

bench	chin	shine	thank

1. This word begins like **shoe** and ends like **line**.
2. This word begins like **boy** and ends like **lunch**.
3. This word rhymes with **win**.
4. This word begins like **thin** and rhymes with **sank**.

Preview Words:
   sh, ch, tch, th, wr, ck

Write a word from the box that is related in meaning to each pair of words.

chuckle	scratches	shower	wrinkle

5. cuts, scrapes
6. storm, downpour
7. fold, crease
8. laugh, giggle

84

Content Words

Science: Human Body

Write the word from the box for each definition.

| lips | wrist | thumb | tongue |

1. part of the mouth used in tasting and swallowing food
2. part of the face that surrounds the mouth
3. the shortest, thickest finger
4. part of the arm that joins the hand

Social Studies: Family

Write the word that completes each sentence.

| brother | family | sister | chores |

I have one ___5.___ named Jed. I have one ___6.___ named Leah. There are no other children in my ___7.___. We all like to play together, but we never do ___8.___ together.

Apply the Spelling Strategy

Circle the **th** or the **ch** in three of the Content Words you wrote.

Word Study

Anagrams

Anagrams are words that have all the same letters, but the letters are in a different order in each word. **Slip** and **lips** are anagrams. Write the Strategy Word that is an anagram of **inch**.

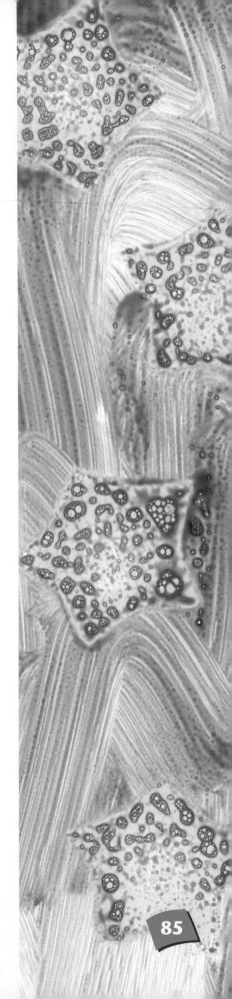

READ THE SPELLING WORDS

1.	change	*change*	I will **change** into my baseball clothes.
2.	fence	*fence*	There is a **fence** around the pool.
3.	space	*space*	We use this **space** as a gym.
4.	age	*age*	Letifa is now ten years of **age**.
5.	center	*center*	My desk is in the **center** of the room.
6.	large	*large*	We ordered a **large** pizza.
7.	since	*since*	I have been able to swim **since** I was five.
8.	price	*price*	The **price** of the book is ten dollars.
9.	page	*page*	Read to the bottom of the **page**.
10.	ice	*ice*	The **ice** will melt when it warms up.
11.	dance	*dance*	Mom and Dad **dance** at the party.
12.	pencil	*pencil*	This **pencil** has no eraser.
13.	slice	*slice*	Please cut me a **slice** of bread.
14.	place	*place*	This is a nice **place** to visit.
15.	city	*city*	We take the bus into the **city**.

SORT THE SPELLING WORDS

1.–4. Write the words that have the **/j/** sound.

5.–15. Write the words that have the **/s/** sound.

REMEMBER THE SPELLING STRATEGY

Remember that the **/j/** sound in **age** is spelled **g**, followed by **e**. The **/s/** sound in **ice** and **city** is spelled **c**. The **c** is followed by **e** (**ice**) or by **i** (**city**).

Sound and Letter Patterns

Write the spelling word for each clue.

1. It begins with the **long a** sound.
2. It has the sound of **s** twice and contains the word **in**.
3. It begins with the **long i** sound.
4. It rhymes with **chance**.
5. It has four letters and two syllables.
6. It has the /**s**/ sound in its second syllable.
7. It has one syllable and the **short e** sound.

Synonyms

Write the spelling word that is a synonym for each of these words.

8. middle
9. cost
10. big

11. put
12. cut
13. area

USING THE Dictionary

The two words at the top of a dictionary page are called **guide words**. The guide word at the left is the first entry word on that page. The guide word at the right is the last entry word on that page. Write the spelling word that would be on the same page as these guide words.

14. over • pepper

15. cavity • children

Spelling and Reading

change	fence	space	age	center
large	since	price	page	ice
dance	pencil	slice	place	city

Use the Clues Write the spelling word that fits each clue.

1. This word can describe an elephant.
2. This is where to find the planets and stars.
3. This names one piece of bread.
4. This means "from then until now."
5. This is a small part of a book.
6. This names a very large town.
7. This is on a package for sale or in a bar code.
8. This word names a waltz or a tango.
9. This word names a country, building, or park.

Complete the Riddles Write a spelling word to answer each riddle.

10. What runs all around a field but never moves? a
    f_____

11. What goes up and never comes down? a_____

12. What is the hardest thing about learning to skate?
    the i_____

13. What makes a point but never says a word? a
    p_____

14. Why did the woman have her pocketbook open?
    She was expecting some c_____ in the weather.

15. Why is a nose always in the middle of a face? It's
    the c_____.

Spelling and Writing

Proofread a Letter

Five words are not spelled correctly in this letter. Write the words correctly.

Dear Neighbors,

   Let's make the playground a better plase for children! We can chang this larje spase into a great park. The fence needs to be fixed also, sinse it fell down in May. We'll meet at my house on Sunday.

                              Yours truly,
                              Mark Jackson

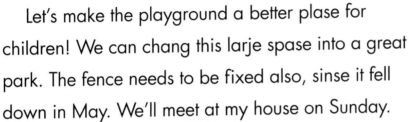

Proofreading Marks

≡	Make a capital.
/	Make a small letter.
∧	Add something.
ℓ	Take out something.
⊙	Add a period.
⌗	New paragraph
SP	Spelling error

Write a Letter

Persuasive Writing

What change would you like to make in your school, neighborhood, or town? Write a letter to friends asking for help. Be sure to tell

- what needs changing.
- what your plans are.
- why others might want to help.

Use as many spelling words as you can.

Proofread Your Writing During ▶ Editing

Proofread your writing for spelling errors as part of the editing stage in the writing process. Be sure to check each word carefully. Use a dictionary to check spelling if you are not sure.

Writing Process

Prewriting
⇩
Drafting
⇩
Revising
⇩
Editing
⇩
Publishing

VOCABULARY CONNECTIONS

►Strategy Words◄

Review Words: Consonants /j/, /s/

Write a word from the box that completes each analogy.

nice	orange	race	spice

1. **Vine** is to **grape** as **tree** is to _____.
2. **Ugly** is to **pretty** as **mean** is to _____.
3. **Rose** is to **flower** as **pepper** is to _____.
4. **Home** is to **apartment** as **contest** is to _____.

Preview Words: Consonants /j/, /s/

Write a word from the box that completes each sentence.

bridge	cellar	engine	piece

5. Please lift the hood of the car so that I can look at the _____.
6. May I cut a _____ of cornbread for you?
7. This large _____ connects northern California to San Francisco.
8. We store cans of food in the _____.

Content Words

Science: Animals

Write the word that matches each description.

| camel | giraffe | zebra | elephant |

1. a humped desert animal that carries loads
2. a large animal with stripes
3. an animal with a long neck, long legs, and short horns
4. the largest land animal

Math: Graphing

Write the word or words that complete each sentence.

| graph | circle | bar | pictograph |

5. A pie chart is round like a _____.
6. When you draw pictures to show items in a chart, you are making a _____.
7.–8. A chart that shows information with blocks of different lengths is a _____ _____.

Apply the Spelling Strategy

Circle the letter that spells the /s/ sound in one of the Content Words you wrote.

Word Study

Word History

Graphein is an old Greek word that meant "to write" or "to draw." Write the Content Word that comes from this word. It means "picture writing."

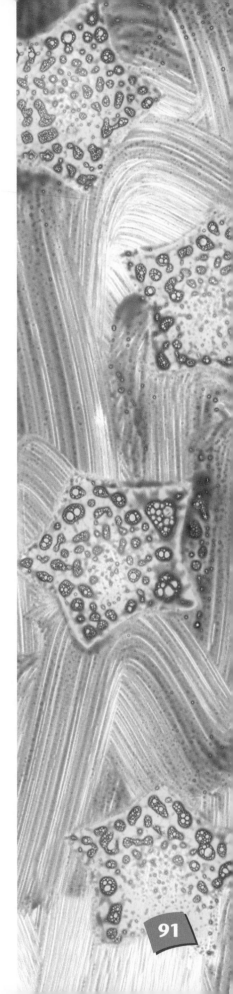

Spelling ^{and} Thinking

READ THE SPELLING WORDS

1. shook	*shook*	I **shook** the juice before pouring it.
2. flash	*flash*	I just saw a **flash** of lightning.
3. speech	*speech*	The mayor made a long **speech**.
4. think	*think*	I like to **think** before I answer.
5. strong	*strong*	We are **strong** enough to lift this.
6. cloth	*cloth*	That coat is made from heavy **cloth**.
7. brook	*brook*	The water in the **brook** is cold.
8. stitch	*stitch*	One **stitch** will not hold the button.
9. string	*string*	The cat chases the ball of **string**.
10. scratch	*scratch*	Please **scratch** my back.
11. fresh	*fresh*	This bread is **fresh** and tasty.
12. spring	*spring*	I will play baseball in the **spring**.
13. switch	*switch*	Use the **switch** to turn on the light.
14. stretch	*stretch*	We want to **stretch** if we sit for too long.
15. splash	*splash*	Jim made a big **splash** in the pool.

SORT THE SPELLING WORDS

1.–12. Write the words with the **sh, ch, tch,** or **ng** digraph.

13.–15. Write the words with the consonant clusters **br, cl,** or **nk**.

REMEMBER THE SPELLING STRATEGY

Remember that **consonant digraphs** are two or more consonants together that spell one new sound: **sh** in **shook**. Two or more consonants together that make more than one sound are called **consonant clusters: br** in **brook**.

Spelling and Phonics

Word Structure

1. Change the last two letters in **flame** to make a spelling word.

2. Delete one letter and change one letter in **strange** to make another spelling word.

3. Change the last three letters in **scraped** to make a spelling word.

4. Change one letter in **stitch** to make another spelling word.

Word Groups

Write the spelling word that belongs in each group.

5. imagine, remember, believe, _____

6. rope, thread, _____

7. winter, summer, fall, _____

8. stream, creek, _____

9. new, clean, _____

10. talk, lecture, sermon, _____

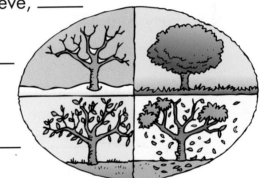

The words in a dictionary are in a-b-c order.

11.–15. Write these words in a-b-c order.

stretch   splash

shook   stitch

cloth

◆ ◆ ◆

Dictionary Check Be sure to check the a-b-c order in your **Spelling Dictionary**.

Spelling and Reading

shook	flash	speech	think	strong
cloth	brook	stitch	string	scratch
fresh	spring	switch	stretch	splash

Solve the Analogies Write a spelling word to complete each analogy.

1. **Mountain** is to **hill** as **river** is to _____.
2. **Tiny** is to **huge** as **stale** is to _____.
3. **Evening** is to **morning** as **fall** is to _____.
4. **Take** is to **took** as **shake** is to _____.
5. **Eye** is to **sight** as **tongue** is to _____.
6. **Easy** is to **difficult** as **weak** is to _____.
7. **Sentence** is to **write** as **idea** is to _____.

Complete the Sentences Write a spelling word to complete each sentence.

8. Use a soft _____ to wipe down the car.
9. Did you see the _____ when you took the picture?
10. Can you _____ your arms up to the ceiling?
11. I got a _____ on my elbow from falling down.
12. The doctor sewed one _____ in Jimmy's finger.
13. Please don't _____ me. I don't want to get wet!
14. You can tie the package with _____.
15. We will _____ schools in sixth grade.

94

Spelling and Writing

Proofread a Paragraph

Five words are not spelled correctly in this paragraph. Write the words correctly.

We hiked up Sugar Mountain on a warm, clear, sping day. We followed the rushing barook to the top. The sun was hot, and there was a storng, frech breeze. We saw hawks in the blue sky and smelled the deep green pine trees. After the hike, I think we were all ready to strech out for a nap!

Proofreading Marks

≡	Make a capital.
/	Make a small letter.
∧	Add something.
ℓ	Take out something.
⊙	Add a period.
⌗	New paragraph
SP	Spelling error

Write a Paragraph

Descriptive Writing

Think of something you did or saw at a fair or a festival that you can describe. Write a paragraph about it. Be sure to include

- details about size, shape, and color.
- words that tell about what you saw, heard, smelled, touched, or, perhaps, tasted.

Use as many spelling words as you can.

Proofread Your Writing During ▶

Writing Process

Prewriting

⬇

Drafting

⬇

Revising

⬇

Editing

⬇

Publishing

Proofread your writing for spelling errors as part of the editing stage in the writing process. Be sure to check each word carefully. Use a dictionary to check spelling if you are not sure.

95

VOCABULARY CONNECTIONS

Strategy Words

Review Words: Digraphs, Clusters

Write a word from the box for each clue.

bring	clap	store	trash

1. It begins like **stop** and ends like **more**.
2. It rhymes with **crash**.
3. It has a /**k**/ sound but no letter **k**.
4. It begins like **brand** and ends like **sing**.

Preview Words: Digraphs, Clusters

Write a word from the box to complete each sentence.

flight	station	strange	thunder

When we went to bed, we were excited about our trip the next day. But when we woke up in the morning, the sky was a ___5.___ gray color. It wasn't long until we heard a clap of ___6.___. We turned on the local radio ___7.___. We found out that the airport was closed. Our ___8.___ to Orlando would not leave today.

Content Words

Science: Ocean Life

Write the word that matches each description.

| starfish | whale | shark | octopus |

1. a sea animal that is shaped like a star
2. a sea animal with a soft body and eight arms
3. the largest of all animals on land or sea
4. a large ocean fish with sharp teeth

Math: Numbers

Write the word from the box that can replace the number or set of numbers in each sentence.

| twenty-four | fifty-nine | thirty-two | sixty-one |

5. I got 59 trading cards for my birthday.
6. There are 61 third graders in our school.
7. My Aunt Sharon is 10 + 10 + 4 years old.
8. My Uncle Jed is 10 + 10 + 10 + 2 years old.

Apply the Spelling Strategy

Circle the **sh** or **wh** digraph in three of the Content Words you wrote.

Word Study

Word Roots

A **root** is a word part. The root **octo** is from a very old word that meant "eight." Write the Content Word that has this root.

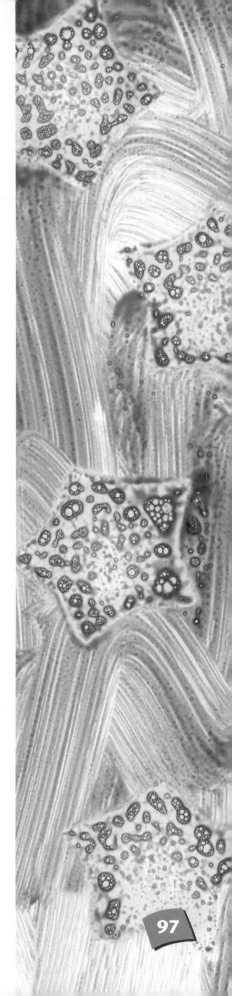

97

Spelling and Thinking

READ THE SPELLING WORDS

1. afraid	*afraid*	Is Cindy **afraid** of that big dog?
2. around	*around*	Let's run **around** the block.
3. upon	*upon*	We looked **upon** a strange sight.
4. never	*never*	You should **never** call people names.
5. open	*open*	May I **open** my presents now?
6. animal	*animal*	The **animal** has four legs and a tail.
7. ever	*ever*	Will we **ever** get there?
8. about	*about*	This book is **about** a hidden cave.
9. again	*again*	We will visit Grandpa **again** tonight.
10. another	*another*	Take **another** look at what you wrote.
11. couple	*couple*	That **couple** has three children.
12. awake	*awake*	Are you **awake** at seven o'clock?
13. over	*over*	I climbed **over** the tall fence.
14. asleep	*asleep*	My dog is **asleep** on his bed.
15. above	*above*	The light switch is **above** the desk.

SORT THE SPELLING WORDS

Write the words that have

    1.–2. more than one **schwa** sound.

    3.–10. just one **schwa** sound, in the first syllable.

    11.–15. just one **schwa** sound, in the last syllable.

REMEMBER THE SPELLING STRATEGY

Remember that the **schwa** sound can be spelled in different ways: **a** in **about, u** in **upon,** and **e** in **over.**

98

Spelling ᵃⁿᵈ Phonics

Sound and Letter Patterns

Write the spelling words by adding the missing letters.

1. __ pon
2. ev __ r
3. __ bo __ t
4. __ sl __ ep
5. __ ro __ nd
6. __ ga __ n
7. co __ pl __
8. n __ v __ r

Rhyming Words

9. Write the spelling word that rhymes with **braid**.

10. Write the spelling word that rhymes with **clover**.

11. Write the spelling word that rhymes with **take**.

12. Write the spelling word that rhymes with **love**.

13. Write the spelling word that rhymes with **mother**.

USING THE Dictionary

Look at these dictionary respellings. Say each word. Write the spelling word for each dictionary respelling.

14. /ăn′ ə məl/

15. /ō′ pən/

◆ ◆ ◆

Dictionary Check Be sure to check the respellings in your **Spelling Dictionary**.

99

Spelling ᵃⁿᵈ Reading

afraid	around	upon	never	open
animal	ever	about	again	another
couple	awake	over	asleep	above

Complete the Story Write spelling words to complete the story.

Yesterday, I went to the Stone Zoo. I had __1.__ been there before. I had heard all __2.__ it, though. Everyone said it was a great place to visit. I wanted to see my favorite __3.__, the lion. We had studied lions and other wild creatures in school. I was worried he would be __4.__ when I got there. But he was wide __5.__ ! When he stood __6.__ a rock and roared, I felt a little __7.__. I was glad there was a high fence all __8.__ his area.

Complete the Sentences Write a spelling word that fits each sentence.

9. I would like _____ glass of milk.
10. Have you _____ met my parents?
11. I will leave the door _____ for you.
12. The ball sailed right _____ the wall.
13. Your name is on the list, right _____ mine.
14. I have seen that movie, but I would like to see it _____.
15. My friends and I should be ready to go in a _____ of minutes.

Spelling and Writing

Proofread an E-Mail Message

Five words are not spelled correctly in this e-mail message. Write the words correctly.

> To: SteinJ@mail.net.com
> From: Joshboy27@kids.net
>
> Dear Uncle Jake,
>
> I had anothur great year in baseball. My team is in the playoffs agen! They are in a couple of weeks. My team nevur, evur gives up. See you at Lum Field uround noon.
>
> Your nephew,
>
> Josh

Proofreading Marks

≡	Make a capital.
/	Make a small letter.
∧	Add something.
ℓ	Take out something.
⊙	Add a period.
⌗	New paragraph
SP	Spelling error

Write an E-Mail Message

Expository Writing

Invite a friend or an adult to come see you in a game, play, or other event. Be sure to tell

- the day.
- the time.
- the place.
- what will happen.

Use as many spelling words as you can.

Writing Process

Prewriting
⇩
Drafting
⇩
Revising
⇩
Editing
⇩
Publishing

Proofread Your Writing During ▶ Editing

Proofread your writing for spelling errors as part of the editing stage in the writing process. Be sure to check each word carefully. Use a dictionary to check spelling if you are not sure.

Unit 16 enrichment

VOCABULARY CONNECTIONS

►Strategy Words◄

Review Words: The Schwa Sound

Write the word from the box that matches each clue.

| model | planted | seven | wagon |

1. This word has the **schwa** sound spelled **o**.
2. This word ends with the **schwa** sound and the letter **l**.
3. This word rhymes with **chanted**.
4. This word has a **short e** sound and the **schwa** sound spelled **e**.

Preview Words: The Schwa Sound

Write the word from the box to complete each meaning-related group.

| agree | alarm | tractor | water |

5. mower, plow, thresher, _____
6. soil, air, _____
7. nod, say yes, _____
8. bell, beeper, buzzer, _____

102

Content Words

Language Arts: Time

Write the word that answers each question.

tomorrow	tonight	yesterday	today

1. What is the day that came before today?
2. What is the day that will come after today?
3. What do you call the day you are in right now?
4. What is today when the sun goes down?

Science: Animal Names

Write the word from the box that matches each clue.

beaver	rabbit	raccoon	skunk

5. animal with sharp teeth that builds dams
6. animal with markings that look like a mask
7. animal that defends itself with a bad smell
8. animal that has long ears and soft fur

Apply the Spelling Strategy

Circle the letter that spells the **schwa** sound in two of the Content Words you wrote.

Word Study

Idioms

An **idiom** is a saying that doesn't mean what the words in it say. **Raining cats and dogs** means that it is raining very hard. Write one Strategy Word to finish all these sayings: **in deep ____; in hot ____; tread ____.**

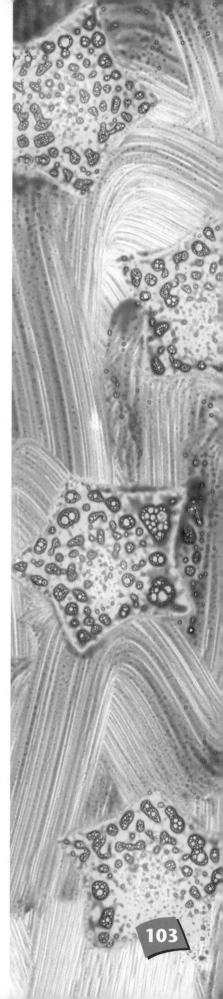

Spelling and Thinking

READ THE SPELLING WORDS

1. friend	*friend*	I play with my **friend** Jonathan.
2. very	*very*	That is a **very** tall building.
3. people	*people*	Many **people** wait in line for tickets.
4. your	*your*	I will give you **your** present.
5. after	*after*	We have gym **after** lunch.
6. busy	*busy*	The **busy** woman worked two jobs.
7. other	*other*	What **other** books have you read?
8. were	*were*	We **were** sleeping when Abe visited.
9. should	*should*	You **should** take off your hat in school.
10. once	*once*	I will ask you this just **once**.
11. would	*would*	No one **would** do such a mean thing.
12. sure	*sure*	Are you **sure** you forgot the key?
13. little	*little*	The **little** boy cried for his mom.
14. every	*every*	Ted ate **every** bite of his dinner.
15. could	*could*	We **could** ride our bikes to the park.

SORT THE SPELLING WORDS

1.–8. Write the words with one syllable.

9.–15. Write the words with two syllables. Draw a line between the syllables.

REMEMBER THE SPELLING STRATEGY

Remember that it is important to learn the spellings of words that writers often misspell.

Word Analysis

Write the spelling word for each clue.

1. This word is inside **another**.
2. It has the /**sh**/ sound and ends with a vowel.
3. In this word, the letters **ie** spell the **short e** sound.
4. It begins with **sh** and rhymes with **could**.
5. It has the /**k**/ sound but no letter **k**.
6. It sounds the same as the word **wood**.
7. It has two syllables. Both begin with the same consonant.

Word Groups

Write the spelling word that belongs in each group.

8. all, each, _____
9. really, a lot, _____
10. later, behind, _____
11. small, tiny, _____
12. twice, never, _____
13. my, his, her, their, _____

USING THE
Dictionary

Write the spelling word that would be on the same page as these guide words.

14. weigh • work
15. bunny • caterpillar

◆ ◆ ◆

Dictionary Check Be sure to check the a-b-c order of the words in your **Spelling Dictionary**.

Spelling and Reading

Replace the Word Replace the underlined part of each sentence with a spelling word.

1. Heather was <u>certain</u> that she had won.
2. Rico is <u>quite</u> proud of his garden.
3. I forgot to study for my spelling test just <u>one time</u>.
4. John is a <u>person I know and like</u>.
5. He knocked on <u>each</u> door.
6. That <u>small</u> dog has a big bark!
7. We will eat dessert <u>following</u> dinner.

Complete the Paragraph Write the spelling words to complete the paragraph.

You __8.__ read about Clara Barton in __9.__ history books. During her lifetime, Clara Barton was a __10.__ woman. She was a teacher, a nurse, and the founder of the American Red Cross. During the Civil War, she __11.__ go out on the battlefield while soldiers __12.__ still shooting at each __13.__. Even after the war ended, she knew she __14.__ do more to help __15.__. That is when she started the American Red Cross.

106

 **Review** Unit 13: sh, ch, tch, th, wr, ck

| father | finish | mother | write | shall | watch | check |

Write the spelling word for each meaning.

1. to end
2. to make letters with a pencil or pen
3. a clock for your wrist
4. a mark for record keeping
5. female parent
6. male parent
7. another word for **will**

 **Review** Unit 14: Consonants /j/, /s/

| change | place | large | since | dance | age | city |

Write the spelling word that completes each sentence.

8. New York is a _____ city.
9. A _____ is larger than a town.
10. I have been out of school ever _____ I caught this bad cold.
11. It is time to _____ the towels.
12. This is the _____ where you should stand.
13. Most children in our town enter school at the _____ of five or six.
14. I love to _____ to that music.

| splash | strong | stretch | think | speech | cloth | shook |

Write the spelling word that rhymes with the underlined word and will complete the sentence.

1. After a <u>dash</u>, I made a _____.
2. This stick is <u>long</u> and very _____.
3. I _____ I will throw this in the <u>sink</u>.
4. He <u>took</u> the jar and _____ out the beans.
5. The creature's _____ sounded like a <u>screech</u>!
6. She got up to _____ after she finished her <u>sketch</u>.
7. Oh, no! There's a <u>moth</u> in the _____.

Review | Unit 16: The Schwa Sound

| again | another | animal | around | about | open | never |

Each spelling word is missing letters. Write each spelling word.

8. __gain
9. an__m__l
10. __round
11. __bout

Write a spelling word for each of these clues.

12. It has two syllables. The first syllable is the **long o** sound.
13. The letter **e** is found in both syllables.
14. The words **not, the,** and **her** can be found in this word.

friend	people	once	would	other	were	could

Write the spelling word that completes each sentence.

1. The girls _____ like to go.
2. Many _____ waited for the bus.
3. That person is my good _____.
4. She was sure that she _____ do it.
5. Bring me the _____ book, not that one.
6. Where _____ you going yesterday?
7. Many stories begin with "_____ upon a time."

GAME Spelling Study Strategy

Spelling Tic-Tac-Toe

Practicing spelling words can be fun if you make it into a game. Here's an idea you can try with a friend.

1. Write your spelling words in a list. Ask your friend to do the same. Trade spelling lists.

2. Draw a tic-tac-toe board on a scrap of paper. Decide who will use **X** and who will use **O**.

3. Ask your partner to call the first word on your spelling list to you. Spell it out loud. If you spell it correctly, make an **X** or an **O** (whichever you are using) on the tic-tac-toe board. If you misspell the word, ask your partner to spell it out loud for you. In that case, you miss your turn.

4. Now you call a word from your partner's list.

5. Keep playing until one of you makes "tic-tac-toe." Keep starting over until you have both practiced all your spelling words.

113

Unit **18** enrichment

Grammar, Usage, and Mechanics

Action Verbs

An action verb tells what the subject of a sentence does or did.

Ellen **caught** the ball.

The dog **barked** at the men.

The whistle **blows** at noon.

A. Write the action verb in these sentences.

1. Her large dog jumped on the couch.

2. The bell rang earlier than usual today.

3. Fish swam around inside the tank.

4. We planted flowers around the porch.

5. Ben sang in the school choir.

B. Write an action verb from the box to complete each sentence.

open	catch	shook	dance	write

6. Juanita will _____ a letter to Dan tomorrow.

7. The stores _____ at noon today.

8. Let's _____ to this music!

9. The wind _____ the tree's branches.

10. He can _____ the baseball.

Proofread a Book Report

Five words are not spelled correctly in this book report. Write the words correctly.

> You should read Arthur's Pet Business. It is by Marc Brown. In this book, Arthur becomes his own bowss. He watches pets that belowng to other people. They pay what he says it will cost. One pet gets lawst. Arthur has to crowl around looking for it. He finds the pet. He also finds something new and saft! This book is fun to read.

Proofreading Marks

≡	Make a capital.
/	Make a small letter.
∧	Add something.
ℓ	Take out something.
⊙	Add a period.
⌗	New paragraph
SP	Spelling error

Write a Book Report

Persuasive Writing

Think of a book you enjoyed. Tell why a friend should read it. Be sure to include

- the title.
- the author.
- one or more reasons to read the book.

Use as many spelling words as you can.

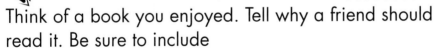

Proofread Your Writing During

Proofread your writing for spelling errors as part of the editing stage in the writing process. Be sure to check each word carefully. Use a dictionary to check spelling if you are not sure.

Writing Process

Prewriting
⬇
Drafting
⬇
Revising
⬇
Editing
⬇
Publishing

119

Unit **19** enrichment

VOCABULARY CONNECTIONS

►Strategy Words◄

Review Words: Vowel /ô/

Write a word from the box for each clue.

dog	jaw	moth	saw

1. This word begins like **job** and ends like **law**.
2. This word rhymes with **hog**.
3. This word begins like **see** and ends like **raw**.
4. This word ends with **th**.

Preview Words: Vowel /ô/

Follow the directions to write each word from the box.

because	bought	caught	haul

5. bite – ite + ought = _____
6. hate – te + ul = _____
7. before – fore + cause = _____
8. catch – tch + ught = _____

120

Content Words

Language Arts: Exact Meanings

Write the word from the box that best replaces each group of underlined words.

rushed	paced	dawdled	dashed

1. Rosa <u>took more time than necessary</u> on the way home.
2. The runner <u>went quickly</u> across the finish line.
3. Todd <u>went with sudden speed</u> to the bus station.
4. The lions <u>went back and forth</u> in the cage.

Health: Teeth

Write the words that best complete the paragraph.

cavity	filling	flossing	crown

Proper brushing and ___5.___ will keep your teeth and gums healthy. If you do get a ___6.___ in the ___7.___ of your tooth, the dentist can give you a ___8.___.

Apply the Spelling Strategy

Circle the letters that spell the /ô/ sound in two of the Content Words you wrote.

Word Study

Word History

This Content Word may have come from an old word, **daddle,** that meant "to walk unsteadily or unevenly." Write the Content Word.

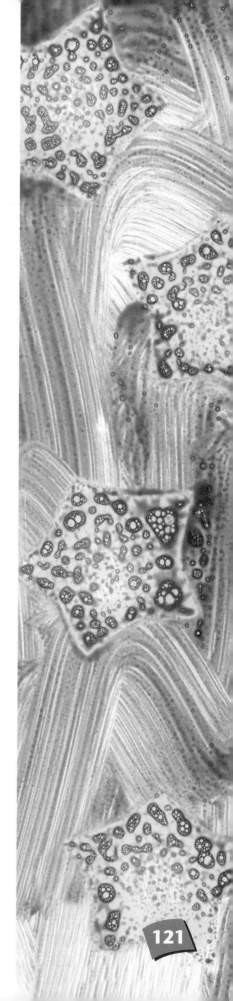

Spelling **and** Thinking

READ THE SPELLING WORDS

1.	story	*story*	Please read me that **story**.
2.	wore	*wore*	Jen **wore** a red dress to the party.
3.	north	*north*	We will head **north** to Canada.
4.	board	*board*	That **board** in the floor is loose.
5.	form	*form*	You can **form** the clay into any shape.
6.	corner	*corner*	Turn left at the next **corner**.
7.	warm	*warm*	You can **warm** up by the fire.
8.	score	*score*	Did Penny **score** the winning goal?
9.	morning	*morning*	Dad gets up early each **morning**.
10.	forget	*forget*	I will not **forget** to drink my milk.
11.	before	*before*	We brush our teeth **before** bed.
12.	storm	*storm*	The noise of the **storm** scared Spot.
13.	tore	*tore*	Matt **tore** his new pants in the game.
14.	order	*order*	May I **order** a hamburger?
15.	war	*war*	We fight the **war** against pollution.

SORT THE SPELLING WORDS

Write the words that spell the /ôr/ sound

1.–4. **ore**.   13.–14. **ar**.

5.–12. **or**.   15. **oar**.

REMEMBER THE SPELLING STRATEGY

Remember that the vowel sound you hear in **form** is
spelled in different ways: **or** in **form**, **ore** in **tore**, **oar** in
board, and **ar** in **warm**.

122

Spelling and Phonics

Sound and Letter Patterns

Write spelling words by adding the missing letters.

1. w __ re
2. t __ r __
3. f __ r __
4. __ t __ rm
5. sc __ r __
6. c __ rn __ r

Word Meanings

Write the spelling word that means the opposite of the underlined word in each sentence below.

7. Tony was a soldier when his country was at <u>peace</u>.
8. The train was traveling <u>south</u>.
9. We will leave early in the <u>evening</u>.
10. Mary arrived <u>after</u> everyone else.
11. Did you <u>remember</u> to bring the map?
12. There was a <u>cool</u> breeze blowing across the lake.

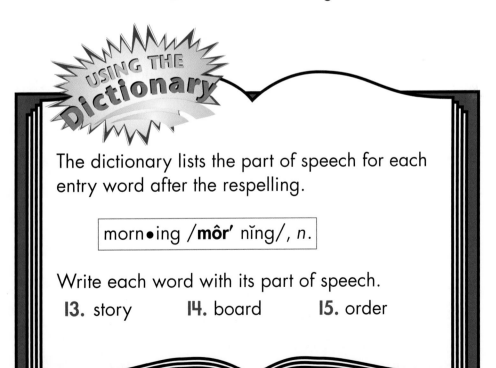

USING THE Dictionary

The dictionary lists the part of speech for each entry word after the respelling.

morn•ing /**môr′** nĭng/, n.

Write each word with its part of speech.

13. story
14. board
15. order

Spelling and Reading

story	wore	north	board	form
corner	warm	score	morning	forget
before	storm	tore	order	war

Name the Categories   Write the spelling word that could name each item in each group.

1. two to one, 23–14, nine to nothing

2. hot dog and fries, one garden salad

3. "Cinderella," "The Three Little Pigs," "Snow White and the Seven Dwarfs"

4. Main Street and Elm Street, Broadway and 34th Street, Michigan Avenue and Rush Street

Complete the Sentences   Write the spelling word that fits each sentence.

5. Kevin _____ a blue sweater and a new pair of shoes to school today.

6. Julie _____ her jacket on the fence at recess.

7. May we have this _____ to finish building our tree house?

8. The boat was damaged during the _____.

9. The dripping water will _____ icicles when it freezes in the cold weather.

10. Ed did not _____ to put a stamp on the letter.

11. I will give you the book _____ you go.

12. Ryan plays tennis in _____ weather.

13. The train tracks are _____ of our house.

14. I hope to see my grandmother bright and early tomorrow _____.

15. My grandfather fought in that _____.

Spelling and Writing

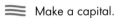

Proofread a Story Beginning

Five words are not spelled correctly in this paragraph. Write the words correctly.

It was early in the morening when Juanita and Tim headed noarth on their search. They woare their old clothes, since the radio had said that a storme was coming. They did not forget their hats. As they turned the last coarner at the edge of town, they saw a man running down the street. He kept looking nervously behind him.

Proofreading Marks

≡ Make a capital.

/ Make a small letter.

∧ Add something.

ℒ Take out something.

⊙ Add a period.

⌗ New paragraph

ⓈⓅ Spelling error

Write a Story Beginning
Narrative Writing

Begin a story in an interesting way. You might even include a hint of mystery, as the writer does above. Be sure to tell

- who is in your story.
- something about the time and place.
- the beginning of the action.

Use as many spelling words as you can.

Proofread Your Writing During ▶ Editing

Writing Process

Prewriting
⇩
Drafting
⇩
Revising
⇩
Editing
⇩
Publishing

Proofread your writing for spelling errors as part of the editing stage in the writing process. Be sure to check each word carefully. Use a dictionary to check spelling if you are not sure.

Unit 20 enrichment

VOCABULARY CONNECTIONS

►Strategy Words◄

Review Words:
r-Controlled Vowel /ôr/

Write a word from the box to complete each group.

corn	horse	more	short

1. wheat, rice, _____
2. plus, in addition, _____
3. small, little, _____
4. goat, cow, donkey, _____

Preview Words:
r-Controlled Vowel /ôr/

Replace the underlined letter or letters to write a word from the box.

forest	forty	report	sport

5. Soccer is my favorite s**h**ort.
6. The teacher asked us to write a rep**air**.
7. Can you swim across the pool f**if**ty times?
8. We enjoyed hiking through the **ar**rest.

Content Words

Science: Plants

Write the word that matches each definition.

branch	thorn	stem	twig

1. a sharp point on a plant
2. a small branch
3. large part of a tree that comes out from the trunk
4. slender part of a plant that supports a leaf, fruit, or flower

Math: Relationships

Write the word that completes each sentence.

even	plus	odd	minus

5. Two _____ seven equals nine.
6. All _____ numbers end in 1, 3, 5, 7, or 9.
7. All _____ numbers end in 2, 4, 6, 8, or 0.
8. Eleven _____ four equals seven.

Apply the Spelling Strategy

Circle the letters that spell the /ôr/ sound in one of the Content Words you wrote.

Word Study

Word Roots

Port was an old word that meant "to carry back" or "to carry information." Write the Strategy Word that is related to this word root and means "a written account."

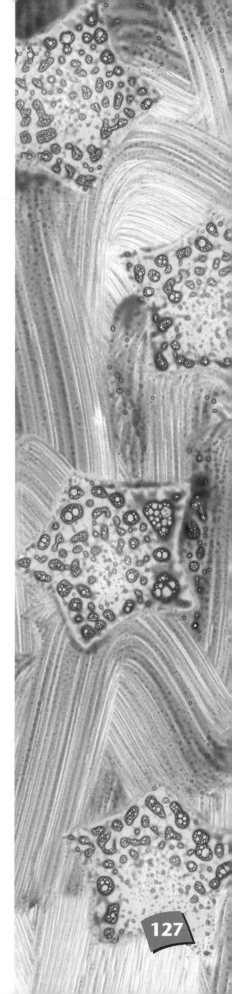

127

Spelling and Thinking

READ THE SPELLING WORDS

1. word	*word*	Be very quiet and do not say a **word**.
2. fur	*fur*	Maria brushed her puppy's soft **fur**.
3. early	*early*	We get up **early** to go to school.
4. circus	*circus*	Keiko saw clowns at the **circus**.
5. turn	*turn*	We took a left **turn** at the stop sign.
6. skirt	*skirt*	I wore my new **skirt** and sweater.
7. earth	*earth*	The **earth** was too wet for planting.
8. work	*work*	They **work** hard caring for the crops.
9. curl	*curl*	How do I **curl** my hair?
10. learn	*learn*	Dad will **learn** to use my computer.
11. hurt	*hurt*	The boy **hurt** his knee when he fell.
12. dirt	*dirt*	Bill digs in the **dirt** for worms.
13. earn	*earn*	The class will **earn** money.
14. shirt	*shirt*	Juan lost a button on his **shirt**.
15. heard	*heard*	Tyler **heard** his mother calling him.

SORT THE SPELLING WORDS

1.–2. Write the words with the /ûr/ sound spelled **or**.

3.–6. Write the words with the /ûr/ sound spelled **ur**.

7.–11. Write the words with the /ûr/ sound spelled **ear**.

12.–15. Write the words with the /ûr/ sound spelled **ir**.

REMEMBER THE SPELLING STRATEGY

Remember that the vowel sound in **fur** is spelled in different ways: **ur** in **fur, ear** in **earn, or** in **word,** and **ir** in **dirt**.

128

Spelling ᵃⁿᵈ Phonics

Word Analysis ━━━━━━━━━━━━━━━━━━━━━━━━

Write the spelling words for these clues.

1.–2. These two words rhyme with **fern** but spell the /ûr/ sound **ear**.

3. This word rhymes with **pearl** but spells the /ûr/ sound **ur**.

4. This word rhymes with **jerk** but spells the /ûr/ sound **or**.

5. This word begins with the /ûr/ sound and ends with **th**.

6. This word has two syllables. The first syllable begins with the /s/ sound spelled **c**.

Sounds and Letters ━━━━━━━━━━━━━━━━━━━

Add the missing letters to write spelling words.

7. __ __ rly   **9.** di __ t   **11.** tu __ n

8. h __ r __   **10.** h __ a __ d

Write the spelling word for each dictionary respelling.

12. /fûr/   **14.** /shûrt/
13. /skûrt/   **15.** /wûrd/

Dictionary Check Be sure to check the respellings in your **Spelling Dictionary**.

Spelling and Reading

word	fur	early	circus	turn
skirt	earth	work	curl	learn
hurt	dirt	earn	shirt	heard

Name the Categories The words below are smaller parts of something bigger. Write the spelling word that names that bigger something.

1. consonants, vowels
2. buttons, collar, cuffs
3. zipper, hem, button
4. hills, plains, mountains
5. clowns, jugglers, elephants

Complete the Story Write spelling words to complete the story.

Do you know what I __6.__? The circus is coming to town! I need to __7.__ some money to buy a ticket. Where can I __8.__? Mr. Ozawa needs help with his garden. Maybe I could help him __9.__ over the soil for planting. I could put the extra __10.__ into flower pots. I would have to start __11.__ in the morning. It will be so cold that I will wish I had a __12.__ coat!

Choose the Word Write the spelling word that fits each clue.

13. It means "harm."
14. It is something you can do to hair.
15. This is what you do in school.

Spelling and Writing

Proofread a Poster

Five words are not spelled correctly in this poster. Write the words correctly.

The Greatest Show on Earth

Have you hurd? The werd is out!

A circous will be held at Jefferson School on Saturday, March 2, at noon.

You can lern more about it and buy your tickets online at www.bellstent.com.

Don't be sorry! Get your tickets urly.

Proofreading Marks

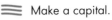 Make a capital.

/ Make a small letter.

∧ Add something.

 Take out something.

 Add a period.

 New paragraph

 Spelling error

Write a Poster

Expository Writing

Make a poster telling about an event at your school or in your town. Be sure to tell

- what is happening.
- where and when it will happen.
- why people should come.

Use as many spelling words as you can.

Writing Process

Prewriting

⇩

Drafting

⇩

Revising

⇩

Proofread Your Writing During ➤ **Editing**

⇩

Publishing

Proofread your writing for spelling errors as part of the editing stage in the writing process. Be sure to check each word carefully. Use a dictionary to check spelling if you are not sure.

131

Spelling and Thinking

READ THE SPELLING WORDS

1. bear	*bear*	The **bear** eats fish and berries.
2. air	*air*	The **air** smells fresh in the forest.
3. fare	*fare*	Do you have change for your bus **fare**?
4. pear	*pear*	Eat the **pear** that is soft and ripe.
5. care	*care*	We will **care** for you if you are sick.
6. their	*their*	They put the food in **their** packs.
7. hair	*hair*	You should brush your **hair**.
8. bare	*bare*	The wind felt cold on Ed's **bare** neck.
9. fair	*fair*	I played a **fair** game and did not cheat.
10. there	*there*	Please place your marker **there**.
11. pair	*pair*	I got a new **pair** of shoes.
12. wear	*wear*	Which hat should I **wear** to the party?
13. chair	*chair*	Kelly sat down in the **chair**.
14. where	*where*	I know **where** to find the lost dog.
15. hare	*hare*	The fox chased the **hare** in the woods.

SORT THE SPELLING WORDS

Write the words that spell the /âr/ sound
1.–5. **air**.
6.–8. **ear**.
9.–12. **are**.
13.–15. **ere** or **eir**.

REMEMBER THE SPELLING STRATEGY

Remember that the vowel sound you hear in **fair** is spelled in different ways: **air** in **fair**, **ear** in **bear**, **are** in **care**, **ere** in **where**, and **eir** in **their**.

Spelling and Phonics

Sound and Letter Patterns

Write spelling words by adding the missing letters.

1. p e __ __
2. t h __ __ r
3. b __ __ e
4. h __ __ r

Sounds and Spellings

5. Write the spelling word that sounds like **hair** but means "a rabbit-like animal."

6. Write the spelling word that sounds like **pear** but means "a set of two."

7. Write the spelling word that sounds like **there** but means "belonging to them."

8. Write the spelling word that sounds like **bare** but means "a large, heavy animal."

9.–12. Write the two pairs of spelling words that sound the same but have different spellings and meanings.

The vowel sound in **pear** is shown as /âr/ in your **Spelling Dictionary**. Write the spelling word for each dictionary respelling.

13. /âr/   14. /kâr/   15. /châr/

◆ ◆ ◆

Dictionary Check Be sure to check the respellings of the words in your **Spelling Dictionary**.

Spelling and Reading

bear	air	fare	pear	care
their	hair	bare	fair	there
pair	wear	chair	where	hare

Complete the Paragraph Write the spelling words that complete the paragraph.

Goldilocks did not have very good manners. She went to the bears' home and ate __1.__ food. She did not __2.__ whose home it was. No matter whose home it was, she should not have been __3.__. Goldilocks sat in each __4.__ in the house. She tried out the bed of each __5.__. One was too hard. One was too soft, but one was just right. She slept in the bed __6.__ she felt most comfortable. It's a wonder she didn't try to __7.__ the bears' clothes!

Complete the Sentences Write a spelling word to complete each sentence.

8. The umpire wants to keep the game _____.
9. Children under twelve pay half _____.
10. A rabbit is sometimes called a _____.
11. Melanie wears her _____ in a braid.
12. I have a new _____ of shoes.
13. Who would like to eat this sweet _____?
14. The grass tickles my _____ feet.
15. It is important to keep our _____ and water clean.

136

Spelling and Writing

Proofread a Paragraph

Five words are not spelled correctly in this paragraph. Write the words correctly.

The Look

What do kids like to wair? They like to put on a peir of jeans and a shirt. Some like their jeans baggy. Some like jeans to fade. Of course, thear are some kids who don't really kare how the jeans look, but they pay a lot of attention to their hare.

Proofreading Marks

≡ Make a capital.

/ Make a small letter.

∧ Add something.

℘ Take out something.

⊙ Add a period.

⌗ New paragraph

(SP) Spelling error

Write a Paragraph

Descriptive Writing

What is in style in your school? Write a paragraph about clothing styles, hair styles, or favorite things to do. Be sure to

- use words that tell what and how.
- give details.

Use as many spelling words as you can.

Writing Process

Prewriting

⇩

Drafting

⇩

Revising

⇩

Proofread Your Writing During ➤ **Editing**

⇩

Publishing

Proofread your writing for spelling errors as part of the editing stage in the writing process. Be sure to check each word carefully. Use a dictionary to check spelling if you are not sure.

137

VOCABULARY CONNECTIONS

Strategy Words

Review Words: r-Controlled Vowel /âr/

Write the word from the box for each clue.

dear	deer	hear	here

1. It ends with the same three letters as **near**. It begins like **day**.
2. It is spelled with the same letters as **hare,** but it does not have the /âr/ sound.
3. It sounds like your answer to number 2, but it has a different spelling and meaning.
4. It sounds like your answer to number 1, but it has a different spelling and meaning.

Preview Words: r-Controlled Vowel /âr/

Follow the directions to write each word from the box.

beware	compare	rare	stare

5. step – ep + are = _____
6. rate – te + re = _____
7. because – cause + ware = _____
8. come – e + pare = _____

138

Content Words

Health: Safety

Write words from the box to complete the paragraph.

| classroom | safety | playground | stairs |

Always follow ___1.___ rules at school. In the ___2.___ stay in your chair. Never run in the halls or on the ___3.___. You can run on the ___4.___, but be careful. Don't run into anyone!

Science: Insects

Write the word from the box that matches each definition.

| caterpillar | wasp | earthworm | housefly |

5. a common worm with a body divided into parts
6. a fly that you may see at home
7. the worm-like, hairy form of a butterfly's life
8. a flying insect that can sting

Apply the Spelling Strategy

Circle the letters that spell the /âr/ sound in one of the Content Words you wrote.

Word Study

Word History

An old French word, **catepelouse,** meant "hairy cat." Write the Content Word that came from this word. It might remind you of a "hairy worm."

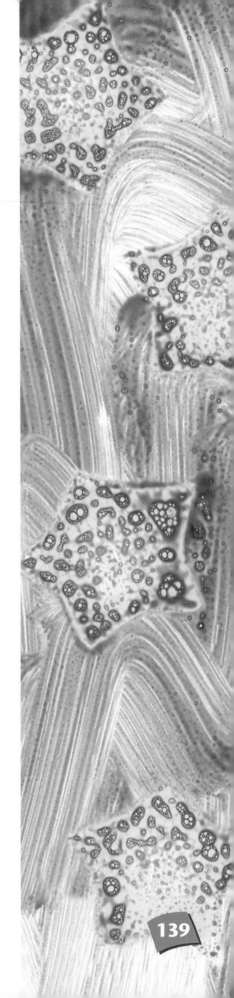

139

Spelling and Thinking

READ THE SPELLING WORDS

1. way	*way*	I don't know which **way** to turn.
2. its	*its*	The dog put **its** head on my lap.
3. owe	*owe*	I **owe** Jay three dollars for the hat.
4. sell	*sell*	If you will **sell** that, I will buy it.
5. great	*great*	What a **great** day we had at the park.
6. sail	*sail*	We **sail** our boat on the bay.
7. cell	*cell*	A **cell** is part of all living things.
8. scent	*scent*	The **scent** of that perfume is strong.
9. oh	*oh*	It was, **oh,** such a beautiful day.
10. cent	*cent*	One **cent** does not buy much!
11. it's	*it's*	I lost my sock, but I know **it's** here.
12. grate	*grate*	Use this tool to **grate** the cheese.
13. weigh	*weigh*	Do you **weigh** the baby on that scale?
14. sale	*sale*	I buy jeans cheap at the **sale**.
15. sent	*sent*	Meg **sent** me a letter from camp.

SORT THE SPELLING WORDS

1.–6. Write the homophones that have the **long a** sound.

7.–11. Write the homophones that have the **short e** sound.

12.–13. Write the homophones that have the **long o** sound.

14.–15. Write the homophones that have the **short i** sound.

REMEMBER THE SPELLING STRATEGY

Remember that **homophones** are words that sound the same but have different spellings and meanings.

Spelling ᴬⁿᵈ Phonics

Word Analysis

Write the spelling words that fit the clues.

1. It spells the /s/ sound with **sc**.
2. It has a **long o** and a **silent h**.
3. It spells the **long a** sound with **ai**.
4.–5. They spell the /s/ sound with **c**.
6. It is spelled with the **vowel-consonant-e** pattern. It begins with **gr**.
7. It begins like **sell** and ends like **cent**.
8.–9. They rhyme with **bits**.

Word Meanings

Write the spelling word that replaces each incorrect homophone below.

10. A store near my house will soon have a <u>sail</u>.
11. It will <u>cell</u> model airplanes at half price.
12. They have such <u>grate</u> prices on model airplanes.
13. Please pay back the money that you <u>oh</u> me.

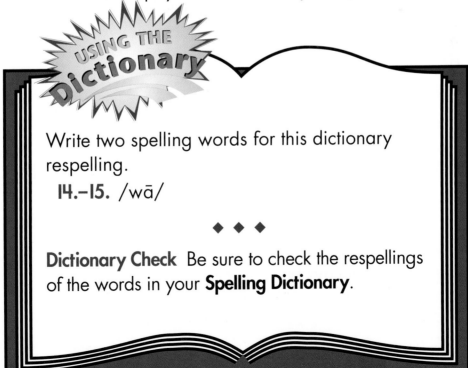

Write two spelling words for this dictionary respelling.

14.–15. /wā/

◆ ◆ ◆

Dictionary Check Be sure to check the respellings of the words in your **Spelling Dictionary**.

way	its	owe	sell	great
sail	cell	scent	oh	cent
it's	grate	weigh	sale	sent

Complete the Groups Write the spelling word that belongs in each group.

1. he's, she's, _____
2. nickel, quarter, dime, _____
3. gee, my, ah, _____
4. fly, drive, ride, _____
5. buy, trade, _____
6. my, her, their, _____
7. chop, shred, _____
8. smell, odor, _____

Complete the Sentences Write the spelling word that fits each sentence.

9. How much does that large bunch of ripe bananas _____?
10. Plants store water in every tiny _____.
11. I _____ you an apology.
12. Our teacher told us that this is the best _____ to solve the math problem.
13. Our whole class had a _____ time on the trip to the science museum.
14. I _____ an e-mail message to my grandmother in Mexico.
15. My dad always buys his clothes on _____.

Spelling ^{and} Writing

Proofread a Paragraph

Five words are not spelled correctly in this paragraph. Write the words correctly.

When a person is missing, sometimes a dog can find the person. It uses it's sense of smell to do this. Someone gives the dog something with the person's sent. Then the dog is cent out to find the person. For many people, its fun to watch a dog pick up the trail. How great it is when the dog can actually find the person. That is when a dog is worth every csent you paid for it!

Proofreading Marks

≡	Make a capital.
/	Make a small letter.
∧	Add something.
ℓ	Take out something.
⊙	Add a period.
#	New paragraph
SP	Spelling error

Write a Paragraph

Expository Writing

Choose one animal and write about it. Be sure to

- write a sentence that tells the main idea of your paragraph.
- use examples, facts, or details to explain the point you are making about the animal.

Use as many spelling words as you can.

Proofread Your Writing During ▶ Editing

Writing Process

Prewriting
⇩
Drafting
⇩
Revising
⇩
Editing
⇩
Publishing

Proofread your writing for spelling errors as part of the editing stage in the writing process. Be sure to check each word carefully. Use a dictionary to check the spelling if you are not sure.

143

Unit 23 enrichment

VOCABULARY CONNECTIONS

Strategy Words

Review Words: Homophones

Write the word from the box that completes each analogy.

for	four	meat	meet

1. **One** is to **two** as **three** is to _____.
2. **Pea** is to **vegetable** as **beef** is to _____.
3. **Wave** is to **greet** as **shake hands** is to _____.
4. **Buy** is to **sell** as **against** is to _____.

Preview Words: Homophones

Write the word from the box that answers each question.

past	passed	roll	role

5. Which word means "time gone by"?
6. Which word means "part in a play"?
7. Which word means "to turn over and over"?
8. Which word means "went by"?

Content Words

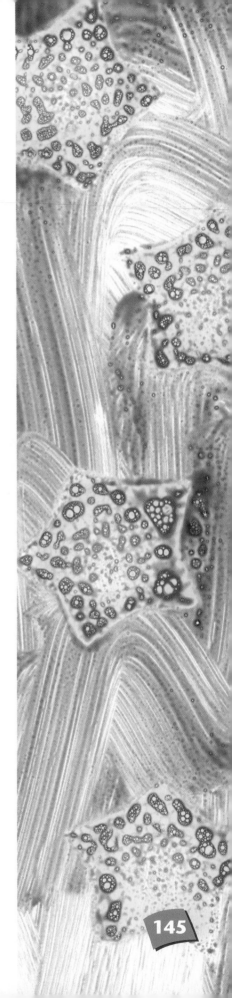

Language Arts: Adjectives

Write the word that completes each sentence.

hungry	chilly	fancy	faraway

1. Other planets are _____ places.
2. Someone who needs food is _____.
3. Things that are not plain might be called _____.
4. You might wear a sweater on a _____ evening.

Science: Medicine

Write the word that matches each definition.

germs	shot	medicine	vaccine

5. tiny cells that can cause disease
6. use of a needle to receive a vaccine or medicine
7. something taken for a disease or injury
8. way of protecting against disease

Apply the Spelling Strategy

Circle the Content Word you wrote that is a homophone for **chili**.

Word Study

Idioms

An **idiom** is a saying that doesn't mean what the words in it say. **Roll up your sleeves** means "get ready to work." Write a Strategy Word to complete this idiom about what you did on a test: _____ **with flying colors**.

145

Each Assessment Word in the box fits one of the spelling strategies you have studied over the past five weeks. Read the spelling strategies. Then write each Assessment Word under the unit number it fits.

Unit 19 _____

1.–3. The vowel sound you hear in **song** and **lawn** is spelled in different ways: **o** in **song** and **aw** in **lawn**.

Unit 20 _____

4.–6. The vowel sound you hear in **form** is spelled in different ways: **or** in **form, ore** in **tore, oar** in **board,** and **ar** in **warm**.

Unit 21 _____

7.–9. The vowel sound in **fur** is spelled in different ways: **ur** in **fur, ear** in **earn, or** in **word,** and **ir** in **dirt**.

Unit 22 _____

10.–12. The vowel sound you hear in **fair** is spelled in different ways: **air** in **fair, ear** in **bear, are** in **care, ere** in **where,** and **eir** in **their**.

Unit 23 _____

13.–15. Homophones are words that sound the same but have different spellings and meanings.

bore

sir

bog

waste

dare

horses

purse

paw

steel

stair

claw

snore

blur

aware

steal

146

**Unit 19: Vowel /ô/**

across	draw	belong	straw	soft	lost	song

Write a spelling word for each one of these clues.

1. It has two syllables and rhymes with **boss**.
2. It rhymes with **cost** and ends with a consonant cluster.
3. It rhymes with **wrong** but has two syllables.
4. Change one letter in **sang** to make this word.

Write a spelling word to complete each sentence.

5. Wipe the car with a _____ cloth so you don't scratch it.
6. Go to the chalkboard and _____ a picture of a cat.
7. We made a bed out of _____ in the doghouse.

Unit 20: r-Controlled Vowel /ôr/

before	forget	warm	morning	story	board	form

Write the spelling word that means the opposite of each word.

8. cool
9. after
10. evening
11. remember

Write a spelling word to complete each sentence.

12. Ms. Bailey told us a _____ about a spider.
13. Dad put a _____ across the muddy walkway.
14. We began to _____ the clay into balls.

147

 Unit 21: r-Controlled Vowel /ûr/

| circus | heard | early | work | turn | dirt | word |

Write the spelling word that completes the sentence.

1. That is a _____ that I have never heard before.

2. Elephants performed in the _____ tent.

3. How _____ can we be ready to leave?

4. I have too much _____ to do to leave tomorrow.

Write a spelling word for each clue.

5. This word rhymes with **burn** and sometimes comes before the word **around**.

6. This word is the past tense of **hear**.

7. Change the first and last letter of **girl** to make this word.

 Unit 22: r-Controlled Vowel /âr/

| their | wear | there | where | chair | bear | care |

Write the spelling word that completes each sentence.

8. My book is over _____ on that table.

9. Joey and Marsha put _____ books in the other room.

10. Do you know _____ to go next?

11. I don't know what to _____ to that party.

12. The little _____ cub stayed close to its mother.

13. You may sit on this _____.

14. Take great _____ not to break this dish.

| great | sent | it's | weigh | cent | oh | its |

Write the spelling word that fits the clue.

1. big or wonderful
2. one way to find out how heavy something is
3. past tense of **send**
4. another name for a **penny**
5. a word of surprise

Write **it's** or **its** to complete each sentence.

6. I hope _____ not too late to go to the game.
7. The poor little kitten has lost _____ mitten.

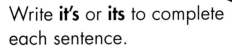 **Spelling Study Strategy**

Sorting by Vowel Sounds

You can practice spelling words by placing them into groups. Here is one way to do that.

1. Write your spelling words on 3" × 5" cards.

2. Make a stack of words that have the vowel sound you hear in **song** and the **r**-controlled vowel sounds you hear in **warm, fur,** and **fair**.

3. With a partner, take turns reading each other's word cards out loud. Put words with the same vowel sound in the same pile.

4. Read the words in each pile again. Then sort them according to the spelling patterns that spell the vowel sound. For example, **word** and **work** would go in the same pile.

Grammar, Usage, and Mechanics

Verbs That Tell About the Past

Past-tense verbs show that the action happened in the past. Many past-tense verbs end in **-ed**.

Yesterday we **worked** in the yard.

The children **played** in the sand.

Some verbs form their past tense in other ways.

We **give** presents on birthdays.

Last year, I **gave** her a book.

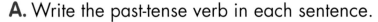

A. Write the past-tense verb in each sentence.

1. Emma listened to her brother's report.
2. Last night my father walked the dog.
3. I finally opened that package!
4. The painter finished the watercolor.
5. The horse jumped over the fence.

B. The underlined verbs below are from your spelling lists in Units 19–23. If a verb is in the past tense, write the word. If it is not in the past tense, write the verb's past-tense form.

6. Those gloves <u>belong</u> to Sal.
7. They <u>work</u> at the food store.
8. Yesterday I <u>heard</u> a robin.
9. Last Monday my teacher <u>sent</u> a note home.
10. The children <u>form</u> clay into bowls.

150

WORKSHOP

Proofreading Strategy

Pair Up with a Partner!

Good writers always proofread their writing for spelling errors. Here's a strategy you can use to proofread your papers.

Ask a partner to read your work aloud slowly, while you check each word. Is it spelled right?

When you hear one word at a time, you notice the spelling more. A partner can also help you fix mistakes. Try it!

Electronic Spelling

Contractions

E-mail is a fast and easy way to keep in touch with people around the world.

Some e-mail programs do not have spell checkers, so you need to be careful to spell words correctly. Be especially careful with contractions. In a contraction an apostrophe takes the place of missing letters.

Which of the underlined contractions below are wrong? Write the word correctly if it isn't. Write **OK** if the word is correct.

1. You go home and <u>Ill</u> call you after school.
2. If <u>your'e</u> going, then I will go.
3. I <u>can't</u> wait for Saturday!
4. My parents <u>wo'nt</u> mind if you come.
5. Please <u>don't</u> forget my mittens.
6. <u>Who'se</u> your favorite baseball player?

Spelling and Thinking

READ THE SPELLING WORDS

1. supper   *supper*   We often have soup for **supper**.
2. happen   *happen*   What will **happen** at the game?
3. pepper   *pepper*   I put **pepper** on my potatoes.
4. kitten   *kitten*   The **kitten** stayed near its mother.
5. sudden   *sudden*   We heard a **sudden** clap of thunder.
6. letter   *letter*   Mail the **letter** at the post office.
7. dinner   *dinner*   We eat rice and beans for **dinner**.
8. cotton   *cotton*   These pants are made from **cotton**.
9. lesson   *lesson*   My piano **lesson** lasts one hour.
10. mitten   *mitten*   I lost one **mitten** in the snow.
11. bottom   *bottom*   The **bottom** of a glass is flat.
12. summer   *summer*   We go to the beach in the **summer**.
13. better   *better*   Colin will feel **better** after a rest.
14. ladder   *ladder*   Climb the **ladder** to reach the window.
15. ribbon   *ribbon*   The bow is made from red **ribbon**.

SORT THE SPELLING WORDS

1.–5. Write the words with a **short u** or **short a** sound.

6.–11. Write the words with a **short e** or **short o** sound.

12.–15. Write the words with a **short i** sound.

REMEMBER THE SPELLING STRATEGY

Remember that two-syllable words with a short vowel sound in the first syllable are often spelled with double consonants: **dinner, better**.

152

Spelling ᵃⁿᵈ Phonics

Sound and Letter Patterns

Write the spelling word that matches each description.

1. It spells the /**k**/ sound with **c**.
2. It has three of the same consonants.
3. It doubles the consonant **b**.
4. It spells the /**k**/ sound with **k**.

Word Structure

Two-syllable words with double consonants in the middle are usually divided between the two consonants. Write these spelling words. Draw a line between the two syllables.

5. bottom
6. better
7. dinner

8. happen
9. mitten

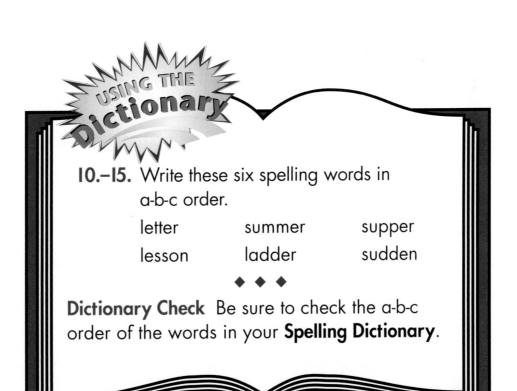

USING THE Dictionary

10.–15. Write these six spelling words in a-b-c order.

letter	summer	supper
lesson	ladder	sudden

♦ ♦ ♦

Dictionary Check Be sure to check the a-b-c order of the words in your **Spelling Dictionary**.

Spelling and Reading

supper	happen	pepper	kitten	sudden
letter	dinner	cotton	lesson	mitten
bottom	summer	better	ladder	ribbon

Complete the Groups Write the spelling word that belongs in each group.

1. silk, wool, _____
2. chili powder, salt, _____
3. scarf, hat, _____
4. occur, take place, _____
5. escalator, steps, _____
6. lunch, brunch, dinner, _____

Complete the Story Write the spelling words to complete the story.

I'll never forget my eighth birthday. It was a very hot __7.__ day. After my swimming __8.__, my mother took me home. I looked in our mailbox and found a birthday card and a __9.__ from my grandparents. Then I went inside. All of a __10.__, my friends yelled, "Happy birthday!" I was so surprised!

We all played games on the __11.__ table. Finally, it was time to open the presents. Mom said I should open the box with holes that was tied with yellow __12.__. Inside was a soft, furry __13.__. It looked so tiny sitting in the __14.__ of that box. I've never gotten a __15.__ present in my whole life!

154

Spelling and Writing

Proofread a Letter

Five words are not spelled correctly in this letter. Write the words correctly.

Dear Kenesha,

My mom just said I could have a sleepover on Friday. This is kind of suden, but can you come? You can have diner here. My mom will make the peper steak that you like! After super, we can play with my kiten. Please answer this letter soon!

Your pal,

Alison

Write a Letter

Persuasive Writing

Invite a friend to do something with you. Be sure to
- use commas after your opening and closing.
- indent your paragraphs, your closing, and your signature.
- persuade your friend with interesting ideas or details.

Use as many spelling words as you can.

Proofread Your Writing During ➤ Editing

Proofread your writing for spelling errors as part of the editing stage in the writing process. Be sure to check each word carefully. Use a dictionary to check spelling if you are not sure.

Writing Process

Prewriting

⇩

Drafting

⇩

Revising

⇩

Editing

⇩

Publishing

155

Unit 25 enrichment

VOCABULARY CONNECTIONS

Strategy Words

Review Words: Double Consonants

Write the word from the box that completes each group.

apple	cannot	puzzle	yellow

1. red, blue, _____
2. maze, riddle, _____
3. plum, peach, _____
4. do not, would not, _____

Preview Words: Double Consonants

Write the word from the box that completes each analogy.

bubble	collar	rattle	zipper

5. **Flower** is to **tulip** as **toy** is to _____.
6. **Water** is to **drop** as **air** is to _____.
7. **Shirt** is to **buttons** as **pants** is to _____.
8. **Wrist** is to **cuff** as **neck** is to _____.

156

Content Words

Social Studies: Government

Write words from the box to complete the paragraph.

United States	president	elect	ballot

Some countries are ruled by kings or queens. Some are ruled by other kinds of leaders. In our country, the ___1.___, we have a ___2.___. The people ___3.___ the president to office by casting a ___4.___.

Science: Machines

Write words from the box to complete the paragraph.

raise	machine	lever	pulley

A simple ___5.___ has very few moving parts. One of these is like a seesaw. It is called a ___6.___. You push one side down to ___7.___ the other side. Another is a wheel and axle used with a rope. That is called a ___8.___.

Apply the Spelling Strategy

Circle the double consonant letters in two of the Content Words you wrote.

Word Study

Coined Words

A **coined word** is made up to name something new. Write the Strategy Word that was coined to name a special fastener on pants or jackets.

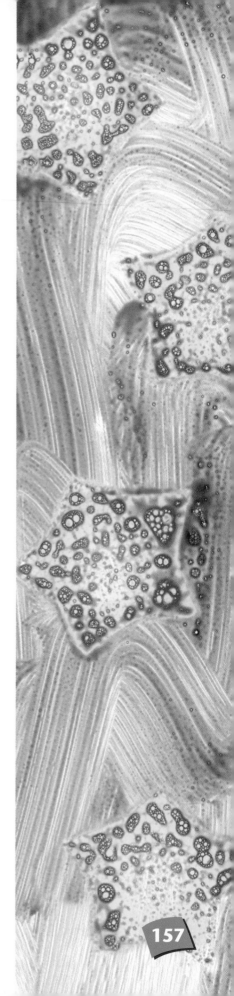

Spelling and Thinking

READ THE SPELLING WORDS

1.	carry	*carry*	Please help me **carry** this box.
2.	bunny	*bunny*	The **bunny** has big ears.
3.	happy	*happy*	The clown made the children **happy**.
4.	muddy	*muddy*	I will take off my **muddy** shoes.
5.	berry	*berry*	What kind of **berry** is on that bush?
6.	furry	*furry*	A hamster is a small **furry** animal.
7.	puppy	*puppy*	The **puppy** is just six weeks old.
8.	sorry	*sorry*	She felt **sorry** for the hurt bird.
9.	merry	*merry*	Everyone at the party was **merry**.
10.	jelly	*jelly*	I eat peanut butter with **jelly**.
11.	hurry	*hurry*	We **hurry** to catch the bus.
12.	pretty	*pretty*	Erica looks **pretty** in that dress.
13.	cherry	*cherry*	This **cherry** is big, red, and ripe.
14.	worry	*worry*	Did Pam **worry** about her lost dog?
15.	funny	*funny*	The joke Matt told was **funny**.

SORT THE SPELLING WORDS

1.–8. Write the words with a **double r**.

9.–10. Write the words with a **double n**.

11.–12. Write the words with a **double p**.

13.–15. Write the words with a **double d, l,** or **t**.

REMEMBER THE SPELLING STRATEGY

Remember that a final **long e** sound in words like **happy** usually follows a double consonant and is spelled **y**.

Word Structure

1. Change one letter in **poppy** to make a spelling word.

2. Replace the second syllable in **sorrow** to make a spelling word.

3. Replace the first syllable in **tidy** to make a spelling word.

4. Change one letter in **jolly** to make a spelling word.

Sound and Letter Patterns

Write spelling words by adding the missing letters.

5. hap ⎯ ⎯

6. bu ⎯ ⎯ y

7. be ⎯ r ⎯

8. f ⎯ n ⎯ y

9. ch ⎯ r ⎯ y

Write the spelling word for each dictionary respelling.

10. /měr′ ē/

11. /fûr′ ē/

12. /wŭr′ ē/

13. /kăr′ ē/

14. /hŭr′ ē/

15. /prĭt′ ē/

Spelling and Reading

carry	bunny	happy	muddy	berry
furry	puppy	sorry	merry	jelly
hurry	pretty	cherry	worry	funny

Replace the Words Write the spelling word that could best replace each underlined word or words.

1. Do you like grape <u>jam</u> on your toast?
2. That <u>baby dog</u> is so playful.
3. "She'll Be Comin' Round the Mountain" is a <u>jolly</u> tune we sing in school.
4. We must <u>be quick</u>, or we will miss the train and lose a day of vacation.
5. I just saw a <u>rabbit</u> eating the lettuce and carrots in our garden.

Complete the Sentences Write the spelling word to complete each sentence.

6. That was a _____ joke you told.
7. It is too _____ to play in the yard.
8. I saw three clowns with _____ faces.
9. Can you help me _____ this heavy package to the post office today?
10. Dad will _____ if we are late for supper.
11. A kitten is soft and _____.
12. I am _____ that I bumped your leg.
13. Look at the _____ flowers.
14. That _____ is so big and blue.
15. A _____ tree has beautiful pink and white blossoms in the spring.

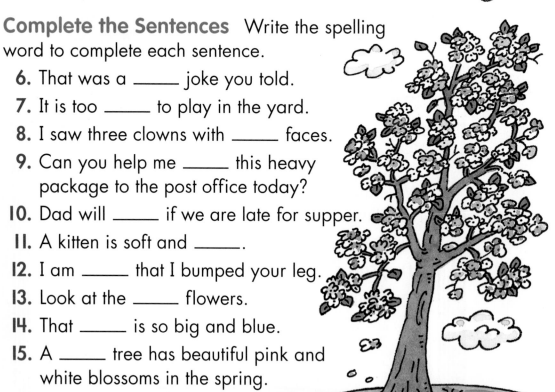

Spelling **and** Writing

Proofread a Thank-You Letter

Five words are not spelled correctly in this letter. Write the words correctly.

Dear Grandma,

   Thank you for the pritty dress. I hope Saturday comes in a hurre because I want to wear it.

   For my birthday I also got a new pack to cary my books. Best of all, Dad got me a pupy.

   It was a very happey day for me. I am sorry you could not be here with me.

                                    Love,
                                    Jemma

Proofreading Marks

- ≡ Make a capital.
- / Make a small letter.
- ∧ Add something.
- ℒ Take out something.
- ⊙ Add a period.
- ⌗ New paragraph
- SP Spelling error

Write a Thank-You Letter

Expository Writing

Write a letter to thank someone for a present or for something the person did for you. Be sure to

- use commas after your opening and closing.
- indent your paragraphs and your closing.
- name the thing you are thanking the person for.
- say something kind about what you received.

Use as many spelling words as you can.

Proofread Your Writing During ▶ **Editing**

Writing Process

Prewriting
⇩
Drafting
⇩
Revising
⇩
Editing
⇩
Publishing

Proofread your writing for spelling errors as part of the editing stage in the writing process. Be sure to check each word carefully. Use a dictionary to check spelling if you are not sure.

Unit 26 enrichment

VOCABULARY CONNECTIONS

Strategy Words

Review Words: Double Consonants + y

Write a word from the box for each clue.

fluffy	glossy	hobby	penny

1. It means "smooth and shiny."
2. An example of it is stamp collecting.
3. It belongs in the same group with the words **dime** and **nickel**.
4. This word could describe fur, feathers, or a blanket.

Preview Words: Double Consonants + y

Write a word from the box to answer each question.

ferry	silly	unhappy	witty

5. Which word tells about a person who is clever at making jokes?
6. Which word describes a happy, giggling feeling?
7. Which word names a type of large boat?
8. Which word describes someone who is wearing a frown?

Content Words

Health: Safety

Write words from the box to complete the paragraph.

| crosswalk | signal | sidewalk | stoplight |

Remember these rules for riding a bicycle in traffic. Always __1.__ before you turn. Stay off the __2.__. Obey any __3.__ you come to. Walk your bike across the __4.__.

Science: Ocean Life

Write the word that matches each definition.

| jellyfish | snake | sea horse | turtle |

5. land animal with a long body and no legs
6. sea animal with a head like a horse and a tail
7. animal that can live on land or water and whose body is covered by a large shell
8. sea animal that can sting

Apply the Spelling Strategy

Circle the Content Word you wrote in which a double consonant is followed by the **long e** sound spelled **y**.

Word Study

Compound Words

A **compound word** is made of two or more smaller words. Write the Content Word that is a compound word meaning "a fish that looks like jelly."

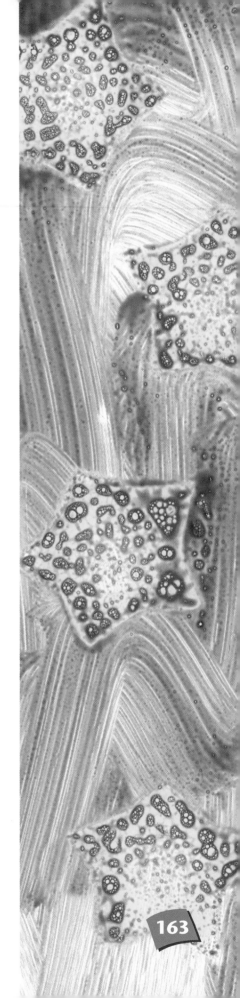

163

Spelling and Thinking

1.	coming	*coming*	Is Zach **coming** to your party?
2.	skating	*skating*	We went ice **skating** at the rink.
3.	taking	*taking*	Ron is **taking** Spot for a walk.
4.	giving	*giving*	Mr. Kay is **giving** me a ride home.
5.	choosing	*choosing*	We are **choosing** a team leader.
6.	smiling	*smiling*	The boys are **smiling** at the clown.
7.	baking	*baking*	I like the smell of bread **baking**.
8.	sliding	*sliding*	Mud is **sliding** onto the road.
9.	changing	*changing*	Is the car **changing** lanes?
10.	waving	*waving*	The flag is **waving** in the breeze.
11.	leaving	*leaving*	Is Ned **leaving** your house?
12.	making	*making*	I am **making** a salad for dinner.
13.	hoping	*hoping*	We are **hoping** you feel better soon.
14.	trading	*trading*	Is that your stack of **trading** cards?
15.	having	*having*	I am **having** a sleepover tonight.

SORT THE SPELLING WORDS

1.–9. Write the spelling words that begin with a consonant followed by a vowel.

10.–15. Write the spelling words that begin with a consonant digraph or consonant cluster.

REMEMBER THE SPELLING STRATEGY

Remember that when you add **-ing** to a word that ends in **silent e,** drop the **e** and add the ending: **take, taking.**

Word Analysis

Write the spelling word that fits each clue.

1. It spells the **long e** sound with **ea**.
2. It spells the **short u** sound with **o**.
3. It has a **short a** sound and looks like **waving**.
4. Change one letter in **living**.
5. It has the **ng** digraph twice.

Rhyming Words

Write the spelling word that completes each sentence and rhymes with the underlined word.

6. The judges are <u>rating</u> each skater's _____.
7. I am <u>raking</u> leaves, and Jan is _____ them away.
8. Fred is <u>making</u> cookies, and Jill is _____ bread.
9. We are _____ to the crew <u>paving</u> the street.
10. The babies keep _____ noise and <u>waking</u> me up.

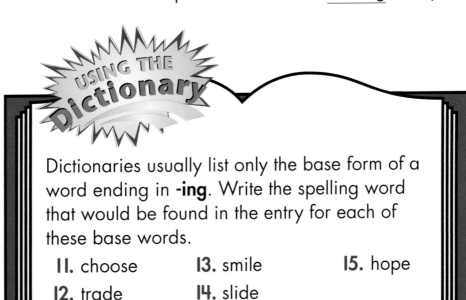

USING THE Dictionary

Dictionaries usually list only the base form of a word ending in **-ing**. Write the spelling word that would be found in the entry for each of these base words.

11. choose
12. trade
13. smile
14. slide
15. hope

Spelling and Reading

coming	skating	taking	giving	choosing
smiling	baking	sliding	changing	waving
leaving	making	hoping	trading	having

Solve the Analogies Write a spelling word to complete each analogy.

1. **Destroying** is to **breaking** as **creating** is to _____.
2. **Leaving** is to **arriving** as **going** is to _____.
3. **Meat** is to **cooking** as **bread** is to _____.
4. **Track** is to **running** as **rink** is to _____.
5. **Sad** is to **frowning** as **happy** is to _____.
6. **Ball** is to **rolling** as **sled** is to _____.

Complete the Sentences Write the spelling word that fits each sentence.

7. I am _____ my new soccer ball for Ann's new basketball.
8. Do you have trouble _____ from a menu?
9. Carlos said he plans on _____ the flat tire on my bike tomorrow.
10. Those old newspapers and magazines are _____ up too much space.
11. Sandy was _____ to get a bicycle for her birthday.
12. I will be _____ early for school tomorrow.
13. We are _____ hamburgers, potatoes, and fresh vegetables for dinner.
14. Gifts are for _____.
15. The children are looking out the window and _____ good-bye to their favorite teacher.

Spelling  Writing

Proofread a Paragraph

Five words are not spelled correctly in this paragraph. Write the words correctly.

The scouts were haveing a meeting after school. Everyone was waiting outside, hopeing that Mary would be comming soon. She was bringing a new member. Suddenly the scouts started making a lot of noise and wavving at a car. It was Mary. Soon everyone was smileing and giving the new member a warm welcome.

Proofreading Marks

☰ Make a capital.

/ Make a small letter.

∧ Add something.

ℓ Take out something.

⊙ Add a period.

⌗ New paragraph

ⓢⓟ Spelling error

Write a Paragraph

Narrative Writing

Write about a time when you waited for someone to arrive or for something to happen. Be sure to tell

- who was there.
- when it happened.
- what happened.

Use as many spelling words as you can.

Proofread Your Writing During ► **Editing**

Proofread your writing for spelling errors as part of the editing stage in the writing process. Be sure to check each word carefully. Use a dictionary to check spelling if you are not sure.

Writing Process

Prewriting

⇩

Drafting

⇩

Revising

⇩

Editing

⇩

Publishing

167

VOCABULARY CONNECTIONS

Strategy Words

Review Words: Adding -ing

Combine each word from the box with **-ing** to make a new word.

grade	drive	live	save

1. grade + ing = _____

2. drive + ing = _____

3. live + ing = _____

4. save + ing = _____

Preview Words: Adding -ing

Write the word from the box that fits each of these clues.

greeting	handwriting	painting	weaving

5. This word is made up of two words.

6. **Watercolor** is an example of this word.

7. **Hello** is an example of this word.

8. **Making a rug** is an example of this word.

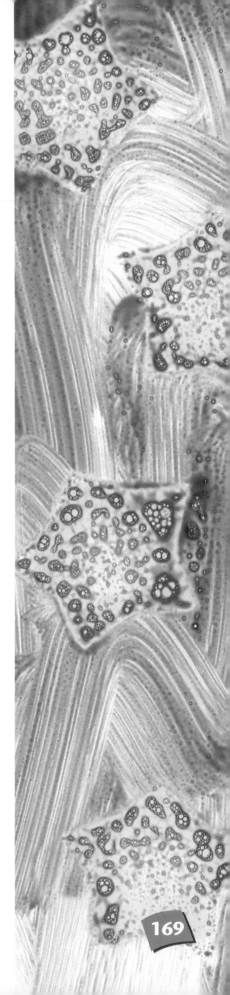

Content Words

Language Arts: Vacations

Write the word that completes each sentence.

camp	trail	cabin	explore

1. We will hike on a _____ in the Rocky Mountains.
2. At the end of the day, we will set up a _____.
3. The next day we will _____ the high country.
4. At the end of the hike, we will rent a _____ in the park.

Social Studies: Manufacturing

Write the word that matches each definition.

factory	goods	mill	trade

5. a building where grain is ground into flour
6. buying and selling
7. a building where furniture is made
8. things that workers make

Apply the Spelling Strategy

Circle the two Content Words you wrote that would drop their final **e** before adding the ending **-ing**.

Word Study

Prefixes

A **prefix** is a word part added to the front of a word. The prefix **ex-** means "out." Write the Content Word that has this prefix and means "to go out to find new places."

Spelling and Thinking

READ THE SPELLING WORDS

1. stopped	*stopped*	The car **stopped** at the stop sign.
2. digging	*digging*	The dog is **digging** a hole.
3. rubbed	*rubbed*	I **rubbed** the cat's back.
4. sitting	*sitting*	Who was **sitting** in my chair?
5. planned	*planned*	We **planned** Mom's birthday party.
6. wrapping	*wrapping*	We are **wrapping** the gift.
7. sledding	*sledding*	Brett went **sledding** on that hill.
8. dropped	*dropped*	Pat **dropped** the bat on my toe.
9. scrubbing	*scrubbing*	Pete is **scrubbing** the pot clean.
10. hopped	*hopped*	The rabbit **hopped** away.
11. putting	*putting*	I am **putting** my shoes on now.
12. tripped	*tripped*	Ari **tripped** over the dog's bone.
13. swimming	*swimming*	We went **swimming** in the pool.
14. spotted	*spotted*	Ty **spotted** an eagle on the cliff.
15. running	*running*	Who is **running** in today's race?

SORT THE SPELLING WORDS

Write the spelling words that
   1.–7. double the consonant and add **-ed**.
   8.–15. double the consonant and add **-ing**.

REMEMBER THE SPELLING STRATEGY

Remember that when you add **-ed** or **-ing** to a word that ends with one vowel and one consonant, double the consonant and add the ending: **stop, stopped**.

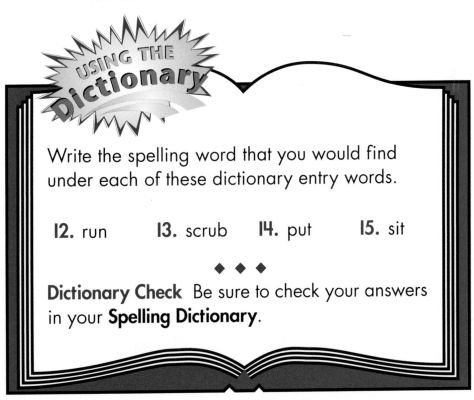

Spelling and Phonics

Beginning and Ending Sounds

Write the spelling words for these clues.

1.–3. Write the spelling words that rhyme with **mopped**.

4.–5. Write the spelling words that begin with consonant clusters with **l**.

Word Structure

6. Write the spelling word that ends with **-ed** and has two syllables.

7. Add one letter to **ripped** to make this word.

8. Take away two letters from **scrubbed** to make this word.

9.–10. Change the first syllables of **hugging** and **stopping** to make these words.

11. Change two letters in **trimming** to make this word.

USING THE Dictionary

Write the spelling word that you would find under each of these dictionary entry words.

12. run   **13.** scrub   **14.** put   **15.** sit

◆ ◆ ◆

Dictionary Check Be sure to check your answers in your **Spelling Dictionary**.

171

Spelling _{and} Reading

stopped	digging	rubbed	sitting	planned
wrapping	sledding	dropped	scrubbing	hopped
putting	tripped	swimming	spotted	running

Edit the Categories Write the spelling word that does not belong in each group.

1. walking, jogging, running, sitting
2. swimming, putting, setting, placing
3. sledding, scrubbing, skating, swimming
4. hopped, jumped, tripped, bounced
5. planned, hoped, stopped, dreamed
6. skated, walked, dropped, jogged
7. hopping, putting, jumping, bouncing

Complete the Sentences Write a spelling word to complete each sentence.

8. Carol _____ her hands together near the campfire to warm them.
9. The dog was _____ a hole in the ground to bury its bone.
10. Roberto likes to go _____ on these steep hills after a snowstorm.
11. A frog _____ in the mud by the pond.
12. Angela _____ to build a doghouse.
13. The cowboy rode a _____ pony in the Fourth of July parade.
14. Kaitlin is _____ after her dog again.
15. We have finished _____ the gifts and making the cookies for the party.

Spelling and Writing

Proofread a Paragraph

Five words are not spelled correctly in this paragraph.
Write the words correctly.

We had a great time at the zoo. We saw sea lions swiming in their tank. We heard the monkeys screaming as they jumped and droped from trees. We saw a spoted snake wrapping itself around a tree trunk. A prairie dog even hoped across our path! That stoped us in our tracks!

Proofreading Marks

≡ Make a capital.

/ Make a small letter.

∧ Add something.

ℓ Take out something.

⊙ Add a period.

⌗ New paragraph

SP Spelling error

Write a Paragraph

Descriptive Writing

Tell about a place you visited. Make it come to life by giving details about what you saw there. Be sure to

- tell what you saw.
- add any other details you observed with your senses, such as things you heard or smelled.

Use as many spelling words as you can.

Writing Process

Prewriting

Drafting

⇩

Revising

⇩

Proofread Your Writing During ➤ **Editing**

⇩

Publishing

Proofread your writing for spelling errors as part of the editing stage in the writing process. Be sure to check each word carefully. Use a dictionary to check spelling if you are not sure.

Strategy Words

Review Words: Adding -ed and -ing

Combine each word from the box with **-ing** to make a new word.

bat	chop	nod	stop

1. nod + ing = _____

2. bat + ing = _____

3. chop + ing = _____

4. stop + ing = _____

Preview Words: Adding -ed and -ing

Write the word from the box that best replaces the underlined word or words.

grabbed	jogging	knitting	strolled

5. Robyn's favorite sport is <u>running</u>.

6. Tom likes <u>making things with yarn and needles</u>.

7. The Ramirez family <u>walked slowly</u> down the avenue.

8. Zoe <u>quickly reached for and held on to</u> the dog's collar before the dog could run away.

| happen | sudden | letter | summer |
| cotton | lesson | better | |

Write the spelling word that completes the sentence.

1. The brakes squealed as the car came to a _____ stop.
2. I studied my science _____ carefully.
3. My teacher says I am doing _____.
4. How could that accident _____?
5. It gets very hot in the _____.
6. My new shirt is made of _____.
7. There was a long _____ from my grandmother in today's mail.

Review **Unit 26: Double Consonants + y**

| funny | pretty | happy | sorry |
| hurry | carry | puppy | |

Write the spelling word that means the opposite of each word or words.

8. ugly
9. sad
10. grown dog
11. glad

Write the spelling word that rhymes with each word.

12. scurry
13. marry
14. honey

baking	having	coming	leaving
taking	giving	changing	

Write the spelling word that completes each sentence.

1. Dad was _____ cookies for our party.
2. Will you be _____ to the party with me?
3. No, I am _____ for the party now.
4. What are you _____ with you?
5. Our picture was taken just as we were _____ Mother the present.
6. We have been _____ a good time.
7. Sit close to me because we are supposed to start _____ places soon.

Review Unit 28: Adding -ed and -ing

dropped	stopped	running	swimming
planned	putting	sitting	

Find the misspelled word in each sentence. Write it correctly.

8. He droped the ball.
9. It was stoppped in time.
10. No runing is allowed at the pool.
11. He was sittin on the porch.
12. Meg planed to go with me.
13. Swiming is my favorite sport.
14. He was puttng away the art supplies.

can't		that's		didn't		won't
	I'm		don't		he's	

Write the spelling word that is a contraction for each word or pair of words below.

1. he is
2. that is
3. will not
4. did not

5. cannot
6. do not
7. I am

GAME

Spelling Study Strategy

Word Swap

Practicing spelling words can be fun if you make it into a game. Here's an idea you can try with a friend.

1. Swap spelling lists with a partner. Ask your partner to read your list and tell you if there are any words she or he doesn't know how to say. Say those words for your partner.

2. Ask your partner to read the first word on your list. Write the word on a piece of scrap paper.

3. Ask your partner to check your spelling. If you spelled the word correctly, your partner should say the next word on your list. If you did not spell the word correctly, ask your partner to spell the word out loud for you. Write the correct spelling.

4. Keep going until you have practiced five words. Then trade jobs. You will say the first word on your partner's list, and she or he will try to write the word correctly. Continue until you and your partner have practiced all the words on your lists.

Unit 30 enrichment

Grammar, Usage, and Mechanics

Adjectives

An adjective describes, or tells about, a noun. Adjectives make sentences more interesting.

A **huge** lizard hid behind the **open** door.

The **hungry** girls quickly ate the **delicious** pizza.

Practice Activity

A. Write the adjective that describes the underlined noun in each sentence.

1. My older <u>brother</u> met me after school.
2. The Florios got a blue <u>van</u>.
3. The sound came from the dark <u>basement</u>.
4. You will need a sharp <u>pencil</u> for this.
5. Be careful with the hot <u>soup</u>!
6. Everyone wants to meet the new <u>teacher</u>.

B. Write an adjective from the spelling lists in Units 25–29 that can complete each sentence.

7. Alan told a very _____ joke!
8. A _____ rainstorm caught us by surprise.
9. Your new dress is so _____!
10. A _____ baby giggles and smiles.

186

WORKSHOP

Proofreading Strategy

Circle and Check

Good writers always proofread their writing for spelling errors. Here's a strategy you can try when you proofread your work.

Instead of reading your whole paper, look at the first three or four words. Are they spelled right? If you are not sure of a word's spelling, circle it. Then go on and check the next group of words. Look at your whole paper this way.

Don't stop to look up words while you're proofreading. Afterwards, you can check the spelling of the circled words. Try it!

Electronic Spelling

Search Engines

Search engines are useful tools. You can type in a word or phrase, and it looks for information about that subject. However, these tools cannot tell if you have misspelled a word. They will look only for the term you type.

Most good searchers type in several forms of a word. For instance, they might type **trucks** and **trucking** and **truckers**. Make sure you spell all the forms correctly.

One word in each pair is wrong. Write it correctly.

1.	story	storyes
2.	woodworkr	woodworking
3.	bakeing	bakers
4.	swiming	swimmers
5.	writers	writeing
6.	cammps	camp

Spelling and Thinking

1. flags   *flags*   That ship is flying two **flags**.
2. inches   *inches*   There are twelve **inches** in a foot.
3. dresses   *dresses*   Pam's **dresses** are all too short.
4. pies   *pies*   Two **pies** are baking in the oven.
5. bushes   *bushes*   The ball is lost in the **bushes**.
6. classes   *classes*   My dad takes **classes** in French.
7. apples   *apples*   Some **apples** fell from the tree.
8. colors   *colors*   What **colors** are in the painting?
9. drums   *drums*   Marge plays the **drums** in the band.
10. branches   *branches*   Some tree **branches** need cutting.
11. things   *things*   I put my **things** in my pack.
12. buses   *buses*   The school **buses** bring us home.
13. benches   *benches*   People sit on **benches** in the park.
14. tracks   *tracks*   We followed the deer's **tracks**.
15. brushes   *brushes*   Those **brushes** are for oil painting.

SORT THE SPELLING WORDS

1.–7. Write the spelling words that form the plural by adding **-s**.

8.–15. Write the spelling words that form the plural by adding **-es**.

REMEMBER THE SPELLING STRATEGY

Remember that you can add **-s** or **-es** to many words to make them plural.

Spelling ᵃⁿᵈ Phonics

Word Analysis

Write the spelling word that fits each clue.

1. It begins with the **short a** sound.

2. It has the letter **o** in both syllables.

3.–4. Their base words end with **ss**.

5. It begins with the **short i** sound.

6. Its base word ends with a single **s**.

Rhyming Words

Write the spelling word that completes each sentence
and rhymes with the underlined word.

7. He <u>tries</u>, but John cannot make apple _____.

8. Lisa <u>hums</u> a tune while Jeremy plays the _____.

9. The skier <u>brags</u>, "I'm the first to pass the _____."

10. My aunt <u>brings</u> lots of funny _____.

11. They loaded their <u>packs</u>, and followed the
    bear's _____.

12. If Matt <u>pushes</u>, he will move the _____.

Guide words help you find words in your
Spelling Dictionary. Write the spelling words
that are on the page with these guide words.

13.–14. bloom • brush   15. bear • blood

◆ ◆ ◆

Dictionary Check Be sure to check the guide
words in your **Spelling Dictionary**.

Spelling and Reading

flags	inches	dresses	pies	bushes
classes	apples	colors	drums	branches
things	buses	benches	tracks	brushes

Complete the Sentences Write the spelling word that completes each sentence.

1. We will need several different sizes of _____ to paint this wall.

2. Orange and red are warm _____.

3. There are many _____ happening at school this week besides classes.

4. A train is coming down the _____.

5. Two _____ are flying on the tall poles in front of our school.

6. Those rose _____ have grown a lot since we planted them last year.

7. There are new _____ on the field for each team's players.

8. Nell is taking ballet _____.

Complete the Groups Write the spelling word that belongs in each group.

9. flutes, pianos, _____

10. miles, yards, feet, _____

11. bananas, peaches, pears, _____

12. cookies, cakes, _____

13. cars, trucks, _____

14. skirts, pants, _____

15. trunks, leaves, _____

Spelling and Writing

Proofread an E-Mail Message

Five words are not spelled correctly in this e-mail message. Write the words correctly.

> To: Lauren2010@edirect.com
> From: Rferrara@fastserve.com
>
> Lauren,
>
> After my brother finishes his clases he will take us to pick apples. Can you come? He wants to see the fall colores, but I just want to follow the rabbit trackes through the bushs. We will have fun. You can eat peies with us later. Write back soon!
>
> Rena

Proofreading Marks

≡ Make a capital.

/ Make a small letter.

∧ Add something.

℮ Take out something.

⊙ Add a period.

⌗ New paragraph

(SP) Spelling error

Write an E-Mail Message

Write an e-mail message inviting someone to go somewhere with you. Be sure to tell

- where you will go.
- when you will go.
- what you will do.

Use as many spelling words as you can.

Writing Process

Prewriting

⇩

Drafting

⇩

Revising

⇩

Proofread Your Writing During **Editing**

⇩

Publishing

Proofread your writing for spelling errors as part of the editing stage in the writing process. Be sure to check each word carefully. Use a dictionary to check spelling if you are not sure.

191

Unit 31 enrichment

VOCABULARY CONNECTIONS

Strategy Words

Review Words: Plurals -s, -es

Write the word from the box that fits each clue.

| boats | foxes | snacks | wishes |

1. It begins like **foot**.
2. It rhymes with **dishes**.
3. It spells the **long o** sound **oa**.
4. It rhymes with **tracks**.

Preview Words: Plurals -s, -es

Write a word from the box to answer each question.

| friends | patches | sandwiches | slippers |

5. What might you use to cover holes in a pair of pants?
6. What might you make for lunch?
7. What might you wear on your feet inside your home?
8. What might you have if you are kind?

Content Words

Language Arts: Fairy Tales

Write words from the box to complete the paragraph.

castle	princess	prince	kingdom

Once upon a time in a faraway land, a __1.__ and a __2.__ lived in a huge __3.__ on a hill. From their tower, they could see the whole __4.__.

Math: Geometry

Write the word that completes each sentence.

endpoints	lines	segments	sides

5. You can draw straight _____ with a ruler.
6. Line _____ are parts of lines.
7. A line segment has two _____.
8. A rectangle has four _____.

Apply the Spelling Strategy

Circle the letters that form the plural in four of the Content Words you wrote.

Word Study

Eponyms

An **eponym** is a word that comes from someone's name. The **leotard** was named after Jules **Leotard,** a trapeze artist. Write the Strategy Word that came from the name **Earl of Sandwich**.

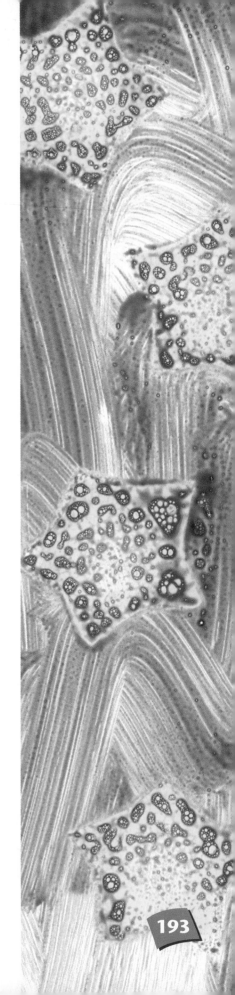

Spelling and Thinking

READ THE SPELLING WORDS

1. goose	*goose*	We cooked a **goose** for dinner.
2. woman	*woman*	The **woman** held her son's hand.
3. calf	*calf*	The **calf** stays near its mother.
4. fish	*fish*	I saw **fish** swimming in the lake.
5. mouse	*mouse*	The **mouse** lives in the hayfield.
6. leaf	*leaf*	A **leaf** takes in light for a plant.
7. children	*children*	The **children** are six years old.
8. geese	*geese*	The **geese** fly together in flocks.
9. calves	*calves*	Many **calves** are in the barn.
10. leaves	*leaves*	The **leaves** fell from the elm tree.
11. half	*half*	We split the orange in **half**.
12. child	*child*	The **child** is looking for her father.
13. women	*women*	These **women** are studying law.
14. mice	*mice*	If **mice** come inside, get a cat.
15. halves	*halves*	Two **halves** make a whole.

SORT THE SPELLING WORDS

1. Write the word that can name both "one" or "more than one."

2.–8. Write the words that name "one."

9.–15. Write the words that name "more than one."

REMEMBER THE SPELLING STRATEGY

Remember that you must change several letters in some words to make the plural form.

Content Words

Language Arts: Nouns and Verbs

Write the word that completes each sentence.

cries	talks	tries	walks

1. The baby is crying. His _____ are loud.
2. I walk to school with Carrie. We enjoy our _____.
3. Jason and I talk often. We have long _____, too.
4. Paula _____ many times before she quits.

Science: Human Body

Write the word that completes each sentence.

cells	organ	nerves	blood

Your heart is an __5.__ that pumps blood. The __6.__ carries oxygen to all parts of your body. Your __7.__ carry messages to and from your brain. Every part of your body is made up of tiny __8.__ .

Apply the Spelling Strategy

Circle the two words in which one or more letters change to make the plural form.

Word Study

Related Words

Related words have the same word or word part in them. For example, **toothbrush** and **toothpaste** are related words. Write the one Strategy Word that relates these words: _____**ball**, _____**hills**, _____**step**.

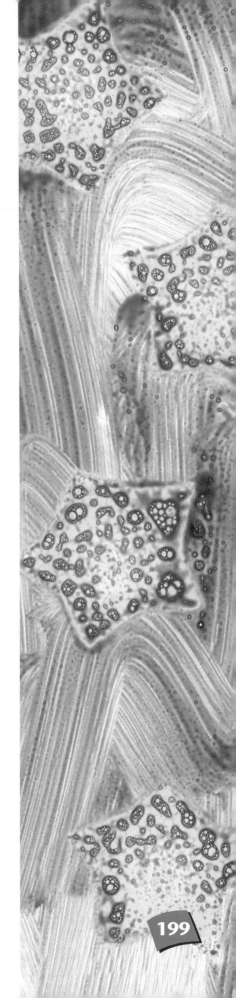

199

Spelling and Thinking

READ THE SPELLING WORDS

1. larger	*larger*	This shoe is **larger** than that one.
2. sadder	*sadder*	Ed is **sadder** than I am.
3. widest	*widest*	I have more room on the **widest** track.
4. sharper	*sharper*	I need to make this pencil **sharper**.
5. closest	*closest*	Leah sits **closest** to the door.
6. hotter	*hotter*	Upstairs is **hotter** than downstairs.
7. saddest	*saddest*	The **saddest** child cried and cried.
8. redder	*redder*	The more he ran, the **redder** he got.
9. reddest	*reddest*	Tara has the **reddest** cheeks of all.
10. wider	*wider*	Trucks can drive on this **wider** road.
11. later	*later*	I will get there **later** than Sue will.
12. largest	*largest*	The whale is the **largest** animal.
13. closer	*closer*	Can you ride **closer** to the fence?
14. hottest	*hottest*	Which frying pan is the **hottest**?
15. latest	*latest*	We listen to the **latest** news on TV.

SORT THE SPELLING WORDS

1.–8. Write the spelling words that end with **-er**.

9.–15. Write the spelling words that end with **-est**.

REMEMBER THE SPELLING STRATEGY

Remember to drop the **silent e** at the end of a word when you add the suffixes **-er** and **-est: wide, wider, widest**. If a word ends in a vowel and consonant, double the consonant when you add **-er** and **-est: hot, hotter, hottest**.

Word Structure

Follow the directions to write a spelling word.

1. late – e + er = _____
2. red + d + er = _____
3. large – e + est = _____
4. hot + t + est = _____
5. close – e + er = _____
6. late – e + est = _____

Beginning and Ending Sounds

Write the spelling word that fits each clue.

7. It begins like **shop**.
8. It begins like **clap** and ends like **best**.
9. It begins like **was** and ends like **after**.
10. It rhymes with **madder**.
11. It begins like **won** and ends like **test**.
12. It rhymes with **gladdest**.
13. It begins like **rock** and ends like **best**.

USING THE Dictionary

Each item below lists an entry word and one spelling word you would find in that entry. Write another spelling word you would find in the same entry.

14. hot, hottest
15. large, largest

◆ ◆ ◆

Dictionary Check Be sure to check your answers in your **Spelling Dictionary**.

Spelling and Reading

larger	sadder	widest	sharper	closest
hotter	saddest	redder	reddest	wider
later	largest	closer	hottest	latest

Add to the Groups Write the word that completes each group of words.

1. sad, _____, saddest

2. wide, wider, _____

3. sharp, _____, sharpest

4. red, redder, _____

Complete the Sentences Write the **-er** or **-est** form of the underlined word that completes each sentence.

5. His <u>red</u> shirt is _____ than mine.

6. That <u>sad</u> clown has the _____ face I have ever seen.

7. Miguel's <u>hot</u> chili is the _____ chili in town.

8. I am <u>late</u> because the bus was _____ than usual.

9. The _____ pig of all is that <u>large</u> one over there.

10. This <u>wide</u> path is _____ than the one behind my house.

Complete the Paragraph Write spelling words from the box to complete the paragraph.

We went to the mall on a hot day. In fact, we couldn't have picked a __11.__ day. It was also a busy day. The __12.__ we got to the mall, the more traffic we saw. The __13.__ we could park our car was in the __14.__ of the two lots. By the time we walked to the stores, it was 5:00. The __15.__ the stores are open is 6:00.

> closest
> latest
> closer
> hotter
> larger

202

Spelling and Phonics

Sound and Letter Patterns

Write spelling words by adding the missing letters.

1. h __ __ rly
2. s __ dd __ nl __
3. bad __ __
4. m __ __ nly
5. __ __ stly
6. cl __ s __ l __

Word Structure

Replace the underlined syllables to make spelling words.

7. plain<u>er</u>
8. slow<u>est</u>
9. short<u>cut</u>
10. soft<u>en</u>
11. loud<u>er</u>

USING THE Dictionary

Write the spelling word that matches each dictionary definition.

12. in part
13. once each month
14. in fact, actually
15. in recent time

◆ ◆ ◆

Dictionary Check Be sure to check the definitions in your **Spelling Dictionary**.

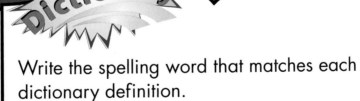

slowly	mainly	badly	hourly	suddenly
lately	partly	closely	really	lastly
plainly	loudly	shortly	monthly	softly

Replace the Words   Write the spelling word that best replaces the underlined word or words.

1. Most cats swim <u>poorly</u>.

2. Have you been to the movies <u>recently</u>?

3. Aesop <u>mostly</u> wrote stories about animals to teach a lesson.

4. I clean my room <u>once a month</u>.

5. Tomatoes are <u>actually</u> fruits, not vegetables.

6. We turned off the lights, closed our eyes, and <u>finally</u> went to sleep.

7. We could <u>clearly</u> see the stars and the full moon in the dark sky.

8. The thunderstorm hit the area <u>quickly and without warning</u>.

9. The train will arrive <u>soon</u>.

Answer the Questions   Write the spelling word that best answers each question.

10. How does a snail crawl?

11. How does a noisy rooster crow?

12. How does a gentle breeze blow?

13. How often does a tower clock usually chime?

14. How was the half-painted house painted?

15. How can you look at things through a microscope?

Spelling and Writing

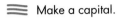

Proofread a Book Report

Five words are not spelled correctly in this book report. Write the words correctly.

The best book I have read lateley is <u>The Magic School Bus Inside a Hurricane</u> by Joanna Cole. The magic school bus changes sudenly into a hot-air balloon. It rises slowly but surely into a storm. The children look closly at how a hurricane forms. Then the bus becomes an airplane, and the children realy have an exciting time. This book is planely not all true, but it is fun to read.

Proofreading Marks

≡	Make a capital.
/	Make a small letter.
∧	Add something.
ℓ	Take out something.
⊙	Add a period.
⌗	New paragraph
SP	Spelling error

Write a Book Report

Expository Writing

Think about a book you liked. Tell about it. Be sure to
- give the title and author of the book.
- tell some details about the book.
- tell why someone else might like it.

Use as many spelling words as you can.

Writing Process

Prewriting

⇩

Drafting

⇩

Revising

⇩

Proofread Your Writing During ▸ Editing

⇩

Publishing

Proofread your writing for spelling errors as part of the editing stage in the writing process. Be sure to check each word carefully. Use a dictionary to check spelling if you are not sure.

VOCABULARY CONNECTIONS

◄Strategy Words►

Review Words: Suffix -ly

Write the word from the box that completes the word math.

cleanly	gladly	neatly	timely

1. glad + ly = _____
2. neat + ly = _____
3. time + ly = _____
4. clean + ly = _____

Preview Words: Suffix -ly

Write a word from the box that fits each clue.

carelessly	carefully	keenly	unfriendly

5. This word has the two suffixes **-ful** and **-ly** added to it.

6. This word begins with **un-** and has the suffix **-ly**.

7. This word has the two suffixes **-less** and **-ly** added to it.

8. This word has the suffix **-ly** but does not begin with **un-**.

Content Words

Social Studies: Building

Write the word that matches each definition.

electric	cement	resources	dam

1. powered by electricity
2. a wall built across a river
3. sources of wealth to a country and to people
4. something that can be mixed with water and then poured to hold other solids together

Health: Feelings

Write the words to complete the paragraph.

healthy	feelings	understand	angry

A friend is someone who can __5.__ your __6.__.
Friends do not get __7.__ over little differences.
Understanding can help to create a __8.__ friendship.

Apply the Spelling Strategy

Circle the two Content Words you wrote to which you could add an **-ly** suffix with one spelling change.

Word Study

Suffixes

The suffix **-y** can cause a word to mean "full of."
Salty means "full of salt." Write the Content Word that means "full of health."

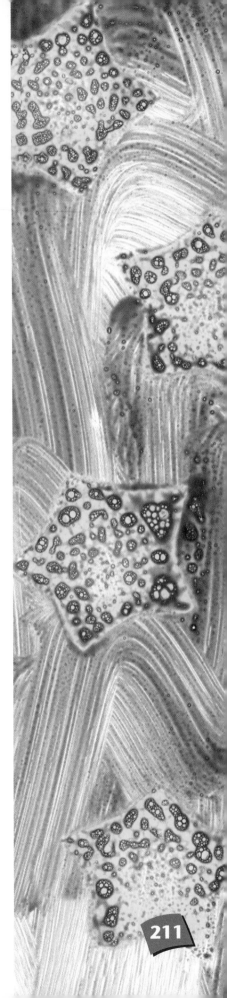

Spelling and Thinking

READ THE SPELLING WORDS

1. herself	*herself*	Li made a cake by **herself**.
2. nobody	*nobody*	There's **nobody** home now.
3. airplane	*airplane*	The **airplane** flies overhead.
4. grandfather	*grandfather*	Our **grandfather** visited us.
5. someone	*someone*	Did you see **someone** run by?
6. rainbow	*rainbow*	We saw a colorful **rainbow**.
7. anything	*anything*	Is there **anything** in the box?
8. grandmother	*grandmother*	My **grandmother** lives here.
9. everything	*everything*	I put **everything** away.
10. afternoon	*afternoon*	I eat lunch in the **afternoon**.
11. sunshine	*sunshine*	The **sunshine** feels warm.
12. himself	*himself*	He drew that **himself**.
13. anybody	*anybody*	Has **anybody** seen my cat?
14. something	*something*	Tell me **something** about him.
15. without	*without*	Don't go out **without** a hat.

SORT THE SPELLING WORDS

1.–11. Write the spelling words in which the first word of the compound word has one syllable.

12.–15. Write the spelling words in which the first word of the compound word has two syllables.

REMEMBER THE SPELLING STRATEGY

Remember that a **compound word** is formed from two or more words: **rainbow, sunshine**.

212

Word Analysis

Two words in each sentence can make a spelling word. Write the word.

1. Pizza is one thing some people love to eat.
2. Julie traded some marbles for one baseball.
3. A book is a thing any library will have.
4. The human body has no tail.
5. Pat went out the door with Aaron.
6. Are there any fish in this body of water?
7. The plane flew high in the air.
8. We left home at noon after we ate.

Word Structure

9.–10. Write the spelling words that begin with **grand**.

11.–12. Write the spelling words that begin with a pronoun and end with the same word.

13. Write the spelling word that begins with **every**.

USING THE **Dictionary**

Guide words help you find words in a dictionary. Write the spelling words that you would find between each pair of guide words.

14. proud • right   15. straw • switch

◆ ◆ ◆

Dictionary Check Be sure to check the guide in your **Spelling Dictionary**.

herself	nobody	airplane
grandfather	someone	rainbow
anything	grandmother	everything
afternoon	sunshine	himself
anybody	something	without

Complete the Sentences Part of a spelling word is missing from one word in each sentence. Add the missing part and write the spelling word.

1. I would give any_____ to visit England.

2. The _____plane was an hour late.

3. My _____father will be sixty-five years old tomorrow.

4. Judy's grand_____ was the first woman doctor in our town.

5. Pam decided to make the dress _____self.

6. Jack looks at _____self in the mirror.

7. The sun_____ always follows the rain.

8. Can you work this _____noon?

9. A rain_____ hung in the clouds for several minutes.

10. Some people lost _____thing in the fire.

Solve the Analogies Write a spelling word to complete each analogy.

11. **All** is to **everybody** as **none** is to _____.

12. **Every** is to **everyone** as **some** is to _____.

13. **Everyone** is to **everybody** as **anyone** is to _____.

14. **Present** is to **absent** as **with** is to _____.

15. **Whole** is to **part** as **everything** is to _____.

214

WORKSHOP

Read Backward

Good writers always proofread their work for spelling errors. Here's a strategy you can use to proofread your writing.

Instead of reading your whole paper from beginning to end, try reading it backward. Start by reading the last word and then the word before it. This way, you would read the sentence, **I read about that man**. like this: .**man that about read I**.

This sounds funny, but reading backward helps you look carefully at each word. You can check spelling without worrying about what the sentence means. Try it!

Electronic Spelling

Searching for Information

Do you ever look for help on-line? You can do this by typing in a word or phrase. Then the computer looks and finds information on that topic. However, it will not find what you want if you misspell the word or phrase that you type.

Many computer terms have **-er** or **-or** endings. Do you know which to use? Find out. Which words below are misspelled? Write them correctly. If a phrase is correct, write **OK**.

1. word processur
2. printor commands
3. enter key
4. text editur
5. eraser tool
6. header and footer

223

Challenge Activities

> packet   magnet   grasp
>
> slim   whiskers

A. Look at the picture and read the small word that names the picture. Then find the small word in a challenge word. Write the challenge word.

1. net   **2.** pack   **3.** whisk   **4.** asp

B. Write a challenge word to complete the sentence. You will write one word twice.

   1. The seeds came in a brown _____.

   2. There is a _____ chance that we will win.

   3. My cat has long white _____.

   4. I can use a _____ to pick up the pins.

   5. My friend is tall and _____.

   6. The pilot will _____ the steering wheel with his hands.

C. Write at least two sentences to answer each question.

   1. What can you pick up with a magnet?

   2. What could you put in a packet?

   3. Who or what can have whiskers?

   4. What might you grasp?

> lemon   welcome   necklace
>
> empty   pocket

A. **1.–2.** Write the two challenge words that contain the letters **c, k,** and **e.**

    3.–5. Write the three challenge words that contain the letters **e** and **m.**

B. Write a challenge word for each clue.

    1. a small bag sewn into clothing

    2. a juicy, yellow, sour fruit

    3. an ornament worn around the neck

    4. the opposite of **full**

    5. to greet with pleasure

C. Think of words or phrases to finish each incomplete sentence. Write your complete sentences. Underline the challenge words.

    1. A lemon tastes _____, but it _____.

    2. I will welcome _____, for my _____.

    3. _____ is now empty, so I can _____.

    4. The necklace was made of _____, and it _____.

    5. The deep pocket was large enough to hold _____ that were _____.

Challenge Activities

trunk	bushel	bucket
ugly	sponge	

A. Some words in the sentences below are missing vowel letters. Write the words correctly.

1.–2. Wash the b __ ck __ t with a sp __ ng __.

3. You can put a b __ sh __ l of apples in it.

4.–5. Do you think the tr __ nk of the tree is __ gly?

B. Write a challenge word to complete each sentence.

1. Caboose is to **train** as _____ is to **car**.

2. Carton is to **eggs** as _____ is to **water**.

3. Gallon is to **milk** as _____ is to **apples**.

4. Straw is to **broom** as _____ is to **mop**.

5. Beautiful is to **princess** as _____ is to **witch**.

C. Write two sentences to answer each question. In the first sentence, just answer the question. For your second sentence, change the underlined word. Use the word in ( ) and answer the new question.

Example: I can't put a giraffe in a large trunk. I can put my favorite toys, books, and photograph album in a large trunk.

1. What can't you put in a large trunk? (can)

2. What wouldn't you clean with a sponge? (would)

3. What isn't put in a bucket? (is)

Challenge Activities

scout	trout	outfit
broil	ointment	

A. Put **oi** or **ou** with the scrambled letters. Unscramble the letters to make challenge words. Write the words.

1. tift + ou = _____
2. mettnn + oi = _____
3. rtt + ou = _____
4. lbr + oi = _____
5. tcs + ou = _____

B. Write a challenge word that can replace the underlined word in each sentence.

1. She wore a new <u>suit</u> to the wedding.
2. The nurse put <u>lotion</u> on the cut.
3. We sent him to <u>search</u> for a new trail.
4. Mom will <u>cook</u> the meat in the oven.
5. My family had <u>fish</u> for dinner.

C. You are with some friends at a camp for a weekend. The bugs are terrible, but the fishing and other lake activities are great. Write about your weekend. Use as many challenge words as possible.

Challenge Activities

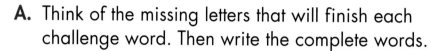

stew	scoop	kangaroo
mushroom	toadstool	

A. Think of the missing letters that will finish each challenge word. Then write the complete words.

1. __ __ oo __

2. __ __ __ __ __ __ oo __

3. __ __ __ __ __ oo __

4. __ __ __ __ __ __ oo

5. Write the challenge word that does not fit in the **oo** pattern.

B. Write the challenge word that goes with each picture. Two different words could go with one picture.

1.   2.–3.   4.   5.

C. A cook is about to reveal his recipe for a world-famous stew. You are a reporter. Write a news article about the cook and the famous stew. Use some challenge words.

Challenge Activities

ripen	siren	grace
erase	shone	

A. Read the sentence. Find a little word hidden in the sentence that is also hidden in a challenge word. Write the challenge word.

   1. A certain time in history is called an era. (The word **era** is in the word **erase**. The answer is **erase**.)

   2. I ask you, sir, did you hear the loud warning?

   3. Will you race me to that tree?

   4. There is only one empty seat.

   5. Be careful not to rip your dress on that fence.

B. Write the missing challenge word that belongs in the sentence.

   1. A cat's movement has natural _____.

   2. My teacher may ask me to _____ the chalkboard.

   3. The fire truck sounded its _____.

   4. Grapes must _____ on the vine.

   5. Last night our flashlight _____ in the darkness.

C. You are interviewing an orange! Think of some questions you may ask it. Think of the answers it might give. Use the challenge words where possible. Write your questions as well as the answers to your questions.

Challenge Activities

> drain   sprain   tailor
> stray   delay

A. Read the rhyming words. Pick one or more challenge words to add to each group. Write the words.

1. paler, trailer, sailor, _____
2.–3. plane, grain, train, _____, _____
4.–5. obey, okay, spray, _____, _____

B. Write a challenge word that can be used in place of each clue.

1. injure
2. pipe
3. one who makes and mends clothes
4. postpone
5. wander

C. The challenge words suggest the five ideas below. Pick one idea and write an explanation. Tell how something happened. (Write the steps in the correct order.)

- what happened to your ankle when you were playing football
- the sink got clogged up
- you were late for school
- your cat got lost
- you (a tailor) made wonderful clothes for a wedding

230

Challenge Activities

peanut	scream	peacock
greet	sleeping	

A. Each challenge word below is missing letters. Think of the missing letters. Then write the complete words.

1. __ ea __ __ __ __

2. __ __ __ ea __

3. __ __ ee __

4. __ __ ee __ __ __ __

5. __ ea __ __ __

B. Three words belong together in each group. Write the one word that does not belong.

1. lemon, peach, pear, peanut

2. talk, scream, say, speak

3. peacock, tuna, shrimp, shark

4. sleeping, playing, running, jumping

5. hands, feet, greet, arms

C. Write a sentence telling about each picture. Use a challenge word in each sentence.

1.

2.

3.

4.

5.

Challenge Activities

nightmare	highlight	grind
	rewind	wildcat

A. Use one part of each word below to form a challenge word. Write the challenge words.

1. flashlight

3. nightingale

2. alley cat

4. refreshments

B. Write a challenge word to answer each question.

1. What might you see in forests or mountains?

2. What might the best part of something be called?

3. What might you do to make flour? You _____ it.

4. What might you have on a bad night?

5. What must you do to your videotape after you watch a movie? You _____ it.

C. You have just awakened from a bad dream. Use some of the challenge words to write about your bad dream.

Challenge Activities

potato	tomato	toast
loaf	swallow	

A. Write the challenge word that each word below suggests to you.

1. gulp
2. juice
3. baked
4. meat
5. breakfast

B. Write the challenge word that matches each definition.

1. to heat or brown by heat
2. commonly grown reddish fruit
3. pass from mouth to throat to stomach
4. vegetable grown underground
5. food baked in one large piece

C. It's four o'clock. You and your older friend want to make a surprise meal for your family. You have two hours. Make a timetable. Write what you will do in those two hours. Use some of the challenge words.

233

Challenge Activities

chance	hatch	seashore
shipwreck	depth	

A. Some letters got into the wrong places in these challenge words. Write each word correctly.

1. sheasore
2. wripsheck
3. ancech
4. tchha
5. thdep

B. Each sentence has a missing challenge word. Write the missing word.

1. My class hopes the eggs will _____ soon.
2. We saw many shells along the _____.
3. The whale can dive to a great _____.
4. You can see the terrible _____ on the rocks.
5. I never take a _____ and cross the street when the light is red.

C. Write a story about a mysterious old ship you found on a nearby coast. Use as many challenge words as you can in your story.

Challenge Activities

> cedar   cider   pounce
>
> plunge   nudge

A. Read the clues below. Write the challenge word that best fits each clue.

1. jump into, rush into
2. juice made from apples
3. reddish wood
4. a little push with the elbow
5. suddenly swoop or jump

B. 1.–5. Proofread the sentence. Find five spelling mistakes. Rewrite each misspelled word correctly.

A tyger was redy too pounse on the dear.

C. Write a short story about a little apple that accidentally got onto the wrong tree. It was a cedar tree, not an apple tree. You may use some of the ideas given below. Put them in your own words. You might pretend you were the apple!

The apple was afraid to go back to its own tree.

A boy down below wanted the apple for a snack.

Challenge Activities

shade	panther	twitch
	crouch	hunger

A. Write the challenge word that goes with the pair.

1. tiger, cheetah

4. shelter, dark

2. stoop, squat

5. thirst, crave

3. tremble, jerk

B. Add **-s** or **-es** to a challenge word to complete each sentence. Write each new word you made.

1. My puppy _____ while he waits for me to throw the ball.

2. A big maple tree _____ our back lawn.

3. The rabbit _____ its nose as it searches for food.

4. Jim reads a great deal because he _____ for knowledge.

5. The three _____ chased the antelopes.

C. Write a fable about a gentle panther that is eating fruits and vegetables as he sits at a table in the shade. Which little animal is nearby? What is it doing? How does it feel? What will the gentle panther do? Use some or all of the challenge words in your fable.

Challenge Activities

award	banana	several
	odor	gorilla

A. Write the challenge words that have these vowel patterns.

1. __ o __ i __ __ a
2. __ a __ a __ a
3. a __ a __ __
4. __ e __ e __ a __
5. o __ o __

B. What am I? Write your answer for each clue.

1. I am an animal in the monkey family.
2. I am more than one.
3. I am a prize.
4. I am a yellow fruit.
5. I am a strong smell.

C. Write a story about one of the pictures. Tell what happened. Use the challenge words where possible.

Challenge Activities

poor	sugar	secret
yourself	o'clock	

A. In this code each letter stands for the letter that comes before it in the alphabet. Write the challenge word for each code word.

Example: bdu = act

1. tvhbs
2. qpps
3. p'dmpdl

4. zpvstfmg
5. tfdsfu

B. Write the challenge word that fits each definition.

1. not good enough
2. pronoun referring to you
3. a sweet substance
4. of or according to the clock
5. something kept from other people

C. You just joined a special club. Using the challenge words, write a story about the first meeting you attend.

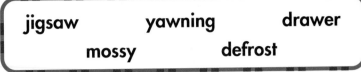

Challenge Activities

Unit 19

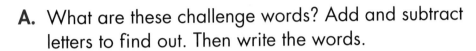

jigsaw	yawning	drawer
mossy	defrost	

A. What are these challenge words? Add and subtract letters to find out. Then write the words.

1. den − n + from − m + last − la = _____
2. day − da + lawn − l + sing − s = _____
3. almost − al − t + easy − ea = _____
4. and − an + raw + her − h = _____
5. j + pig − p + sat − t + w = _____

B. Write a challenge word to complete each sentence.

1. The rocks along the stream were _____.
2. Dad used his _____ to cut out the design.
3. I put my clean clothes in my dresser _____.
4. I knew my sister was tired because she was _____.
5. Mom had to _____ the car's windshield.

C. Imagine that you had a very strange dream. Use some of the challenge words to write about your dream.

239

Challenge Activities

glory	hoarse	boredom
warn	warp	

A. Unscramble these challenge words. Write the words correctly.

1. r o l g y   4. r a w p

2. r a w n   5. s o a r e h

3. d o o r m e b

B. Write the challenge word that fits each definition.

 1. low or rough in sound or voice

 2. to bend or buckle from dampness

 3. a weary feeling because something is not interesting

 4. to tell of coming danger

 5. great honor or praise

C. Choose one of these questions and write two or more sentences to answer it.

 1. What might make a person hoarse?

 2. What might a person have done to receive praise or glory?

 3. When might you have to warn others?

 4. Which things can warp?

Challenge Activities

curve	worm	pearl
	twirl	whirl

A. Use every second letter to decode these challenge words. Start with the second letter. Write the words you find.

Example: abtiprotihedmaly = birthday

1. ptrwaitrel
2. swootrame
3. twaheipralt
4. speekadrill
5. schubraveer

B. What challenge word does each picture make you think of?

1.
2.
3.

4.
5.

C. You own a very talented worm. It can do many tricks. Tell about your pet worm. Write a short story using challenge words.

Challenge Activities

armchair	barefoot	farewell
	fairy tale	somewhere

A. These "words" are not quite right. Correct these misspelled homophones. Write the challenge words. You'll write one word twice.

1. bearfoot   3. fairy tail   5. armchare
2. somewear   4. fairwell   6. ferry tale

B. What word do these pictures suggest? Say the picture words. Then write a challenge word that sounds the same.

1.

3.

2.

4.

C. Make a hidden word puzzle on a grid that has ten squares across and down. Use any spelling words you have studied this school year. Give it to a friend to find the words. Here is an example of how to begin.

a	i	d			
g	c				
e	e				

Challenge Activities

shopping	spinning	planning
hugged	wrapped	

A. Write the **-ed** form for each of these base words.

   I. hug

   2. wrap

B. Write the **-ing** form for each base word.

   I. shop

   2. plan

   3. spin

C. Write the correct **-ed** or **-ing** form for each underlined word.

   I. I am going <u>shop</u> with my parents tonight.

   2. He <u>hug</u> his new brown puppy.

   3. Our family is <u>plan</u> a trip this summer.

   4. The birthday gift was <u>wrap</u> neatly.

   5. Rumpelstiltskin was <u>spin</u> straw into gold.

D. Pretend you went to a birthday party last week. Tell what you did before the party. Then tell about the party. Use as many challenge words as you can.

couldn't	they're	they've
weren't	we're	

A. Write the contraction that is a short form for each word pair.

1. we are   4. they have

2. were not   5. they are

3. could not

B. 1.–5. Five contractions are missing from the story. Read the story. Write the correct contractions.

Alice and Adrienne were born on the same day. In fact, ___1.___ twins. Since kindergarten, ___2.___ attended our school. Alice hoped to be in our homeroom this year, but it ___3.___ be arranged. Adrienne is in our room, and ___4.___ happy about that. We like Alice, too, so we ___5.___ pleased that she is in another class. Maybe next year we will have Alice with us, and we will not have Adrienne!

C. Your class is having difficulty finding a way to raise money for a class trip. Using your challenge words, write a paragraph describing the problem. Then tell how you solved the problem.

Challenge Activities

hoofs	roofs	scarfs
	switches	walruses

A. Finish each sentence. Write plural forms.

1.–2. The two words whose plurals are formed with **-es** are _____ and _____.

3.–5. The three words whose plurals are formed with just **-s** are _____, _____, and _____.

B. Write challenge words to identify the pictures.

1.

4.

2.

5.

3.

C. Mr. Walrus was sitting quietly at home watching TV when a sudden noise outside disturbed him. Use the challenge words to write a short story about what happened.

Challenge Activities

tuna	oxen	elf
elves	popcorn	

A. What are these challenge words? Write them.

1. boxer − b − r + n = _____
2. eat − at + lift − i − t = _____
3. spot − s − t + p + corner − er = _____
4. stun − s − n + nap − p = _____
5. motel − mot + paves − pa = _____

B. Write a challenge word to answer each question.

1. Which strong beasts can pull heavy loads?
2. What might you put in a deep bowl for a TV snack?
3. What is often put in salads or sandwiches?
4. Which make-believe being is said to have magical powers?
5. Who are supposed to be Santa's helpers?

C. What might little elves be doing? Where might they go? Could they help someone? How? Write a story about what the little creatures decide to do.

Spelling Strategy
When You Take a Test

1 **Get** ready for the test. Make sure your paper and pencil are ready.

2 **Listen** as your teacher says each word and uses it in a sentence. Don't write before you hear the word **and** the sentence.

3 **Write** the word carefully. Make sure your handwriting is easy to read. If you want to print your words, ask your teacher.

6 **Circle** any misspelled parts of the word.

4 **Use** a pen to check your test. Look at the word as your teacher says it.

7 **Look** at the correctly written word. Spell the word again. Say each letter out loud.

5 **Say** the word aloud. Listen as your teacher spells the word. Say each letter aloud. Check the word one letter at a time.

8 **Write** any misspelled word correctly.

Spelling Strategy
When You Write a Paper

1 **Think** of the exact word you want to use.

2 **Write** the word, if you know how to spell it.

3 **Say** the word to yourself, if you are not sure how to spell it.

4 **Picture** what the word looks like when you see it written.

5 **Write** the word.

6 **Ask** yourself if the word looks right.

7 **Check** the word in a dictionary if you are not sure.

SPELLING AND THE Writing Process

Writing anything—a friendly letter, a paper for school—usually follows a process. The writing process has five steps. It might look like this if you tried to draw a picture of it:

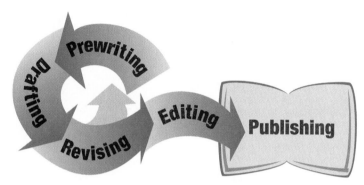

Part of that writing process forms a loop. That is because writers often jump back and forth between the steps as they change their minds and think of new ideas.

Here is a description of each step:

Prewriting This is thinking and planning ahead to help you write.

Drafting This means writing your paper for the first time. You usually just try to get your ideas down on paper. You can fix them later.

Revising This means fixing your final draft. Here is where you rewrite, change, and add words.

Editing This is where you feel you have said all you want to say. Now you proofread your paper for spelling errors and errors in grammar and punctuation.

Publishing This is making a copy of your writing and sharing it with your readers. Put your writing in a form that your readers will enjoy.

SPELLING AND Writing Ideas

Being a good speller can help make you a more confident writer. Writing more can make you a better writer. Here are some ideas to get you started.

Ideas for Descriptive Writing

You might…

- describe something very, very small and something very, very big.
- describe something from the point of view of an insect.
- describe your most prized possession.

Ideas for Narrative Writing

You might…

- write a story about your first visit to someplace new.
- write a story about an event that helped you "grow up."
- write a story about a bad day or a best day playing your favorite sport.

Ideas for Persuasive Writing

You might…

- try to persuade your classmates to read a book you like.
- try to persuade your parents to let you have a pet.
- try to persuade your teacher to change a class rule.

Ideas for Expository Writing

You might…

- write how to prepare your favorite food dish.
- inform your classmates how to create a craft object.
- write instructions on how to care for a pet.

More Ideas for Expository Writing

You might…

- find out how your local government works and write a report.
- interview an animal caregiver and write a report about the job.
- choose a career you might like and write a report about it.

Manuscript Handwriting Models

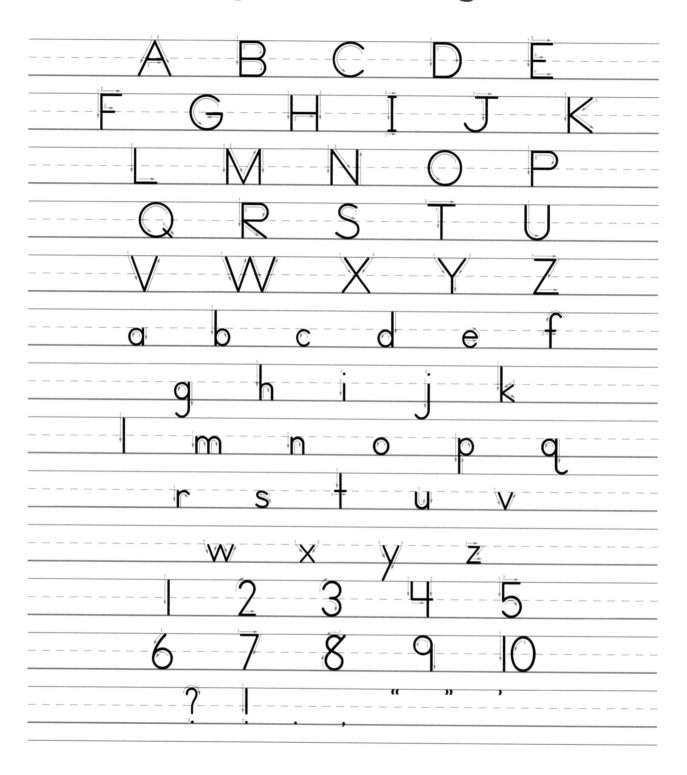

Cursive Handwriting Models

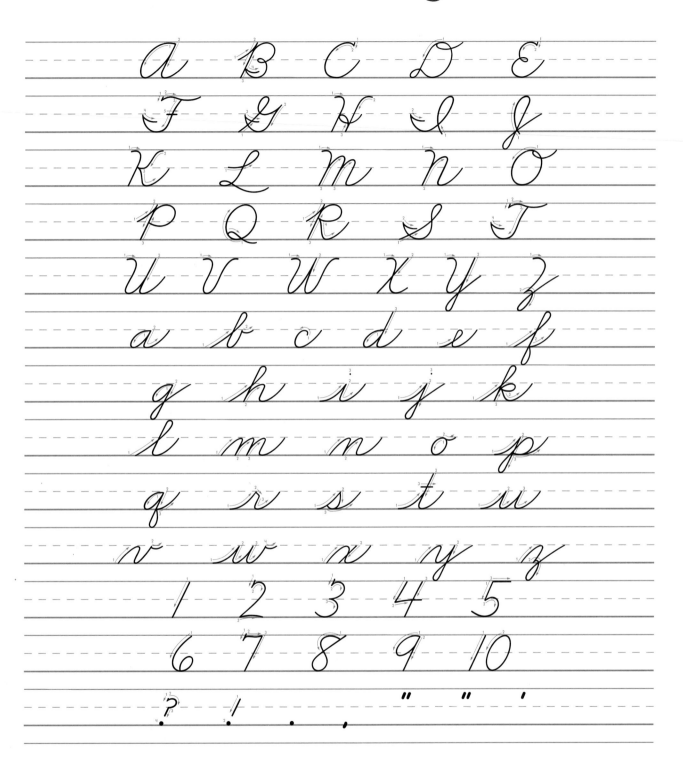

High Frequency Writing Words

A

a
about
afraid
after
again
air
all
almost
also
always
am
America
an
and
animal
animals
another
any
anything
are
around
as
ask
asked
at

ate
away

B

baby
back
bad
ball
balloons
baseball
basketball
be
bear
beautiful
because
become
bed
been
before
being
believe
best
better
big
bike
black
boat

book
books
both
boy
boys
bring
broke
brother
build
bus
but
buy
by

C

call
called
came
can
candy
can't
car
care
cars
cat
catch
caught

change
charge
children
Christmas
circus
city
class
clean
clothes
come
comes
coming
could
couldn't
country
cut

D

Dad
day
days
decided
did
didn't
died
different
dinner

do
does
doesn't
dog
dogs
doing
done
don't
door
down
dream

E

each
earth
eat
eighth
else
end
enough
even
every
everybody
everyone
everything
except
eyes

F

family
fast
father
favorite
feel
feet
fell
few
field
fight
finally
find
fire
first
fish
five
fix
food
football
for
found
four
free
Friday
friend
friends
from

front
fun
funny
future

G

game
games
gas
gave
get
gets
getting
girl
girls
give
go
God
goes
going
good
got
grade
grader
great
ground
grow

H

had
hair
half
happened
happy
hard
has
have
having
he
head
heard
help
her
here
he's
high
hill
him
his
hit
home
homework
hope
horse
horses
hot

hour
house
how
hurt

I

I
I'd
if
I'm
important
in
into
is
it
its
it's

J

job
jump
just

K

keep
kept
kids

killed
kind
knew
know

L

lady
land
last
later
learn
leave
left
let
let's
life
like
liked
likes
little
live
lived
lives
long
look
looked
looking
lost

lot
lots
love
lunch

M

mad
made
make
making
man
many
math
may
maybe
me
mean
men
might
miss
Mom
money
more
morning
most
mother
mouse
move

Mr.
Mrs.
much
music
must
my
myself

N

name
named
need
never
new
next
nice
night
no
not
nothing
now

O

of
off
oh
OK
old

on
once
one
only
or
other
our
out
outside
over
own

P

parents
park
party
people
person
pick
place
planet
play
played
playing
police
president
pretty
probably

problem
put

R

ran
read
ready
real
really
reason
red
responsibilities
rest
ride
riding
right
room
rules
run
running

S

said
same
saw
say
scared
school

schools
sea
second
see
seen
set
seventh
she
ship
shot
should
show
sick
since
sister
sit
sleep
small
snow
so
some
someone
something
sometimes
soon
space
sport
sports

start
started
states
stay
still
stop
stopped
store
story
street
stuff
such
sudden
suddenly
summer
sure
swimming

T

take
talk
talking
teach
teacher
teachers
team
tell
than

Thanksgiving
that
that's
the
their
them
then
there
these
they
they're
thing
things
think
this
thought
three
through
throw
time
times
to
today
together
told
too
took

top
tree
trees
tried
trip
trouble
try
trying
turn
turned
TV
two

U

united
until
up
upon
us
use
used

V

very

W

walk
walked
walking
want
wanted
war
was
wasn't
watch
water
way
we
week
weeks
well
went
were
what
when
where
which
while
white
who
whole
why

will
win
winter
wish
with
without
woke
won
won't
work
world
would
wouldn't

Y

yard
year
years
yes
you
your
you're

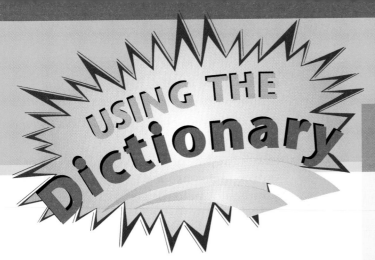

USING THE Dictionary

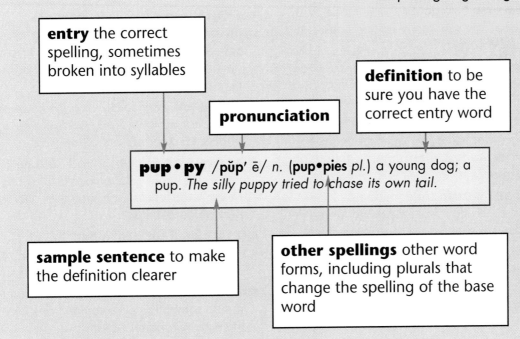

Tips for Finding a Word in a Dictionary

- Practice using guide words in a dictionary. Think of words to spell. Then use the guide words to find each word's entry. Do this again and again until you can use guide words easily.

- Some spellings are listed with the base word. To find **angrier**, you would look up **angry**. To find **planned**, you would look up **plan**. To find **classes,** you would look up **class**.

- If you do not know how to spell a word, guess the spelling before looking it up. Try to find the first three letters of the word. (If you just use the first letter, you will probably take too long.)

- If you can't find a word, think of how else it might be spelled. For example, if a word starts with the /**k**/ **sound,** the spelling might begin with **k** or **c**.

Guide Words

The **guide words** at the top of each dictionary page can help you find the word you want quickly. The first guide word tells you the first word on that page. The second guide word tells you the last word on that page. The entries on the page fall in alphabetical order between these two guide words.

Entries

Words you want to check in the dictionary are called **entries**. Entries have a lot of information besides the correct spelling. Look at the sample entry below.

entry the correct spelling, sometimes broken into syllables

pronunciation

definition to be sure you have the correct entry word

pup • py /pŭp′ ē/ *n.* (**pup•pies** *pl.*) a young dog; a pup. *The silly puppy tried to chase its own tail.*

sample sentence to make the definition clearer

other spellings other word forms, including plurals that change the spelling of the base word

267

A

a•bout¹ /ə bout'/ *prep.* of; having to do with; concerning. *Let me tell you something about baseball.*

a•bout² /ə bout'/ *adv.* somewhere near. *She guessed it was about seven o'clock.*

a•bove¹ /ə bŭv'/ *adv.* in a higher place. *The plane was flying far above.*

a•bove² /ə bŭv'/ *prep.* higher than; over. *The plane went above the clouds.*

a•cross¹ /ə krôs'/ or /ə krŏs'/ *adv.* from side to side. *The room is twenty feet across.*

a•cross² /ə krôs'/ or /ə krŏs'/ *prep.* to the other side of. *The bridge goes across the river.*

act¹ /ăkt/ *n.* a division of a play. *Most plays today have three acts.*

act² /ăkt/ *v.* to perform. *Many girls would like to act in the movies.*

a•do•be¹ /ə dō' bē/ *n.* brick made of baked clay and straw. *Many pueblos are built of adobe.*

a•do•be² /ə dō' bē/ *adj.* made of adobe. *We saw many adobe houses in New Mexico.*

a•fraid /ə frād'/ *adj.* frightened; filled with fear. *Some people are afraid of falling from high places.*

af•ter /ăf' tər/ *prep.* **a.** behind. *Don't forget that you come after me in the parade!* **b.** following; later in time than. *After lunch let's go on with the game.*

af•ter•noon /ăf' tər nōōn'/ *n.* the part of the day that follows noon and lasts until evening. *Little children often take naps in the afternoon.*

a•gain /ə gĕn'/ *adv.* once more. *When no one answered the door, the mailman rang the bell again.*

age /āj/ *n.* number of years old. *The baby's age is now two years.*

aid¹ /ād/ *v.* to help. *The doctor aided him promptly.*

aid² /ād/ *n.* **a.** assistance. *Send aid at once to the men lost in the cave.* **b. first aid** quick help for the injured. *Girl Scouts learn first aid.*

air /âr/ *n.* **a.** the mixture of gases surrounding the earth. *All people breathe air.* **b.** the space above the earth. *Birds and airplanes fly in the air.*

air•plane /âr' plān'/ *n.* a machine for flying that has a motor, wings, and a tail. *The airplane will land in ten minutes.*

airplane

a•like¹ /ə līk'/ *adj.* similar; without a difference. *The twin sisters look alike.*

a•like² /ə līk'/ *adv.* in the same way. *You can't treat all children alike.*

al•most /ôl' mōst'/ or /ôl mōst'/ *adv.* nearly; just about. *That bus is almost on time; it is only two minutes late.*

al•ways /ôl' wāz/ or /ôl' wĕz/ *adv.* all the time; constantly. *At the North Pole, it is always cold.*

an•gry /ăng' grē/ *adj.* (**an•gri•er, an•gri•est; an•gri•ly** *adv.*) feeling or showing anger; filled with anger. *He became angry when he spilled ink on his homework.*

an•i•mal /ăn' ə məl/ *n.* a living being that is not a plant. *Dogs, worms, elephants, and snakes are all animals.*

an•oth•er /ə nŭth' ər/ *adj.* **a.** one more. *Let me read another story.* **b.** any other; a different. *I am going to another part of the country.*

an•y•bod•y /ĕn' ē bŏd' ē/ or /ĕn' ē bŭd' ē/ *pron.* any person. *Did you see anybody that I know at the meeting?*

an•y•thing /ĕn' ē thĭng'/ *pron.* any thing; something. *We couldn't find anything for Grandma's birthday.*

Spelling Dictionary

ap•ple /ăp′ əl/ *n.* a fruit for eating, usually round, that grows on a tree. *Green apples are often used in pies.*

a•round¹ /ə round′/ *prep.* **a.** in a circular path about. *We rode around the block on our bikes.* **b.** on every side of. *There was nothing but water around us.*

a•round² /ə round′/ *adv.* in a circular path. *The merry-go-round went around.*

a•sleep¹ /ə slēp′/ *adj.* not awake; sleeping. *The dog is asleep after a long walk.*

a•sleep² /ə slēp′/ *adv.* into a state of sleep. *He fell asleep during the movie.*

a•wake /ə wāk′/ *adj.* alert; not asleep. *She was already awake when the alarm clock rang.*

a•way /ə wā′/ *adv.* **a.** from a place; to a different place. *Our dog ran away last week.* **b.** aside; out of the way. *He put the dishes away after supper.*

bad•ly /băd′ lē/ *adv.* poorly; in a bad manner. *He plays the piano well but sings badly.*

bake /bāk/ *v.* (**bakes, baked, bak•ing**) to cook without applying fire directly; to cook in an oven. *We bake bread every week.*

bal•loon /bə lōōn′/ *n.* a brightly colored rubber bag that can be filled with air or gas and used as a toy. *Can you blow up this balloon?*

band /bănd/ *n.* **a.** a number of persons who play musical instruments together. *She plays the drums in a band.* **b.** any flat strip of material used for holding something together. *Put a rubber band around each newspaper.*

band

Pronunciation Key

ă	pat	ŏ	pot	th	**th**in
ā	pay	ō	toe	th	**th**is
âr	care	ô	paw, for	hw	**wh**ich
ä	father	oi	noise	zh	vision
ĕ	pet	ou	out	ə	about,
ē	be	ŏŏ	took		item,
ĭ	pit	ōō	boot		pencil,
ī	pie	ŭ	cut		gallop,
îr	pier	ûr	urge		circus

bang¹ /băng/ *n.* a sudden, sharp noise. *We heard the bang of the car door.*

bang² /băng/ *v.* to strike with noisy blows. *Will you please stop banging those pots and pans?*

bar /bär/ *n.* **a.** a long, evenly shaped piece of something solid. *I went to the store for a bar of soap.* **b.** a solid rectangle used to show an amount on a graph. *Color the longest bar on the graph red.*

bare /bâr/ *adj.* **a.** not wearing clothes; not covered. *Should you be walking outside in your bare feet?* **b.** without a covering. *The floor is bare because the rug is being cleaned.*

▶ **Bare** sounds like **bear**.

bay /bā/ *n.* a part of a large body of water that extends into the land; a gulf. *Several small boats came into the bay to escape the storm.*

be /bē/ *v.* (**am, are, is; was, were; been; be•ing**) used as a helping verb in addition to having the following meanings: **a.** to have the identity of; to equal. *Carlos is my cousin.* **b.** to have a particular quality, appearance, or character. *The sand was hot.* **c.** to happen; to take place. *The finals are at two o'clock.*

beach /bēch/ *n.* (**beach•es** *pl.*) the shore of a lake, sea, etc., usually of sand or small stones, that is washed by waves. *During the summer we go to the beach.*

bear /bâr/ *n.* a large, heavy animal with long, coarse fur, short legs, and a very short tail. *The bear stood on its hind legs.*

▶ **Bear** sounds like **bare.**

beat[1] /bēt/ *v.* (**beats, beat•en** or **beat, beat•ing**) **a.** to hit again and again. *Beat the drum loudly.* **b.** to throb. *Her heart was beating fast.* **c.** to defeat. *Linda beat Don in the election.*

beat[2] /bēt/ *n.* a throbbing sound. *Listen to the beat of the drum.*

bea•ver /bē′ vər/ *n.* a furry animal with strong, sharp teeth, a broad, flat tail, and webbed hind feet. *Beavers are noted for building dams.*

beaver

be•come /bĭ kŭm′/ *v.* (**be•comes, be•came, be•come, be•com•ing**) to develop into; to come or grow to be. *A caterpillar may become a butterfly or a moth.*

bee /bē/ *n.* a small insect that gathers pollen from plants and lives in a colony. *Bees make honey and wax.*

beep[1] /bēp/ *n.* a short, high-pitched sound. *The horn gave a loud beep.*

beep[2] /bēp/ *v.* to make such a sound. *My watch beeps once every hour.*

bees•wax /bēz′ wăks′/ *n.* the wax made by bees. *Beeswax is used for making candles.*

be•fore[1] /bĭ fôr′/ *prep.* at an earlier time than. *I had to be home before six o'clock.*

be•fore[2] /bĭ fôr′/ *adv.* previously; at an earlier time. *Have you heard this story before?*

be•fore[3] /bĭ fôr′/ *conj.* earlier than the time when; previous to the time that. *Before you cross the street, look both ways.*

be•long /bĭ lông′/ or /bĭ lŏng′/ *v.* **a.** to have a proper place. *Pots and pans belong in the kitchen.* **b. belong to** to be the property of someone. *The bike belongs to Anita.*

be•low[1] /bĭ lō′/ *adv.* beneath; in a lower place. *Far below, we could see the bottom of the pit.*

be•low[2] /bĭ lō′/ *prep.* in a lower place than; to a lower place than. *Kansas is below Nebraska on the map.*

bench /bĕnch/ *n.* (**bench•es** *pl.*) a long, low, wooden or stone seat that sometimes has a back. *George fell asleep on a bench in the park.*

ber•ry /bĕr′ ē/ *n.* (**ber•ries** *pl.*) **a.** a small, juicy fruit with soft flesh and many seeds. *We had berries and ice cream for dessert.* **b.** the dry seed of certain plants. *The seed used in making coffee is a berry.*

bet•ter /bĕt′ ər/ *adj.* higher in quality; more excellent; finer. *Does anyone have a better plan?*

birch /bûrch/ *n.* (**birch•es** *pl.*) **a.** a tree with smooth bark and hard wood. *Birches grow in North America and Europe.* **b.** the wood of this tree. *Much furniture is made of birch.*

blind[1] /blīnd/ *adj.* not able to see. *Many blind persons know how to read braille.*

blind[2] /blīnd/ *n.* a window shade. *Please raise the blind and let in the sunshine.*

block /blŏk/ *n.* **a.** a solid piece of wood, stone, metal, etc. *Children play with blocks.* **b.** a part of a town or city surrounded by four streets. *The new shopping center covers a city block.*

blood /blŭd/ *n.* the red liquid that flows through the bodies of people and animals. *Blood carries food and oxygen and carries away waste products.*

bloom¹ /blo͞om/ n. the flower of a plant. *The rose is a fragrant bloom.*

bloom² /blo͞om/ v. to have flowers. *Fruit trees bloom in April and May.*

blow /blō/ v. (**blows, blew, blown, blow•ing**) **a.** to move rapidly. *We could hear the wind blow.* **b.** to be moved or stirred by the wind. *The falling leaves are blowing around.* **c.** to cause to make a sound by forcing air through. *Blow the horn again.*

board¹ /bôrd/ or /bōrd/ n. **a.** a long, flat piece of sawed wood. *Boards are used in building houses.* **b.** a flat piece of wood or other material used for a special purpose. *The game of checkers is played on a board.*

board² /bôrd/ or /bōrd/ v. to get on a plane, train, ship, or bus. *The passengers waited to board the airplane.*

boil /boil/ v. **a.** to bubble and send out steam. *When water is heated enough, it boils.* **b.** to heat a liquid until bubbles rise. *He boiled the soup.* **c.** to cook in boiling water. *My mother boiled eggs for breakfast.*

bor•der /bôr′ dər/ n. **a.** an outer edge. *The cabin was built on the border of the forest.* **b.** the imaginary line that divides one state or country from another. *We crossed the border when we visited Canada.*

bor•row /bŏr′ ō/ or /bôr′ ō/ v. to get something to use for a while before returning or repaying it. *May I borrow your spelling book?*

boss /bôs/ or /bŏs/ n. (**boss•es** pl.) the person in charge; the manager. *A good boss knows how to get along with people.*

bot•tom¹ /bŏt′ əm/ n. the lowest part. *The sled flew to the bottom of the hill.*

bot•tom² /bŏt′ əm/ adj. lowest. *Look on the bottom shelf for your book.*

Pronunciation Key

ă	pat	ŏ	pot	th	thin
ā	pay	ō	toe	th	this
âr	care	ô	paw, for	hw	which
ä	father	oi	noise	zh	vision
ĕ	pet	ou	out	ə	about,
ē	be	o͝o	took		item,
ĭ	pit	o͞o	boot		pencil,
ī	pie	ŭ	cut		gallop,
îr	pier	ûr	urge		circus

branch /brănch/ n. (**branch•es** pl.) **a.** a limb of a tree, growing from the trunk or from another limb. *Children climb the branches of large trees.* **b.** a division of a large thing. *This small stream is a branch of the main river.*

break /brāk/ v. (**breaks, broke, bro•ken, break•ing**) **a.** to come apart; to separate into pieces. *Fine china breaks easily.* **b.** to fail to keep or carry out. *Don't break the rules.* **c.** to go beyond; to do better than. *Will the runner break the record?*

breath /brĕth/ n. the air breathed into the lungs and then let out. *Take a deep breath.*

bright /brīt/ adj. **a.** shining; giving light; reflecting light. *See how bright the car is when it is polished.* **b.** clear; brilliant. *She wore a bright red dress.*

broke /brōk/ past tense of **break**.

brook /bro͝ok/ n. a small stream of water. *The children waded in the brook.*

broth•er /brŭth′ ər/ n. a boy or man having the same parents as another person. *The girl had three brothers.*

brush¹ /brŭsh/ n. (**brush•es** pl.) the stiff hairs, straw, wire, etc., set in a stiff back or attached to a handle. *I have a new comb and brush.*

brush

brush² /brŭsh/ v. to smooth or clean with a brush. *Brush your teeth after eating.*

bun•ny /bŭn′ē/ *n.* (**bun•nies** *pl.*) a pet name for a rabbit. *We saw a bunny hiding in the bushes.*

burn¹ /bûrn/ *v.* **a.** to be on fire. *We watched the logs burn.* **b.** to destroy by heat or fire. *The city burns its garbage.* **c.** to damage or hurt by fire, heat, wind, etc. *The sun burned her arms.*

burn² /bûrn/ *n.* an injury or sore made by something very hot. *He had a burn on his finger from the hot stove.*

bus /bŭs/ *n.* (**bus•es** *pl.*) a large motor vehicle that can carry many passengers. *We take a bus to school.*

bush /bŏŏsh/ *n.* (**bush•es** *pl.*) a plant smaller than a tree, with many branches growing near the ground; a shrub. *Roses grow on bushes.*

bus•y /bĭz′ē/ *adj.* (**bus•i•er, bus•i•est; bus•i•ly,** *adv.*) **a.** at work; active. *We will be busy until dark cleaning up the backyard.* **b.** full of work or activity. *The first day of school is always busy.*

buzz¹ /bŭz/ *n.* the humming sound made by some insects. *The country air was still except for the buzz of the bees among the flowers.*

buzz² /bŭz/ *v.* to make a humming sound. *The wasps buzzed around their nest.*

cab•in /kăb′ ĭn/ *n.* a small house, often built of logs. *Abraham Lincoln lived in a cabin.*

calf /kăf/ *n.* (**calves** *pl.*) a young cow. *The calf was only three days old, so he stayed close to his mother.*

calves /kăvz/ plural of **calf**.

cam•el /kăm′ əl/ *n.* a large animal with one or two humps on its back. *Camels can go without drinking water for many days.*

camel

camp¹ /kămp/ *n.* a place in the country where people live in tents or in simple buildings. *My sister goes to camp every summer.*

camp² /kămp/ *v.* to live outdoors for a time, especially in a tent. *On our trip we camped out every night.*

can /kăn/ or /kən/ *v.* (**could**) **a.** to be able to. *A cheetah can run fast.* **b.** to know how to. *Susan can play the drums.*

can't /kănt/ cannot.

care¹ /kâr/ *n.* **a.** protection; close attention. *A baby needs loving care.* **b.** anxiety; concern; worry. *Too much care can cause health problems.*

care² /kâr/ *v.* (**cares, cared, car•ing**) **a.** to feel anxiety, interest, or worry. *I don't care who wins.* **b.** to love or like someone. *He cares deeply for his children.*

car•ry /kăr′ ē/ *v.* (**car•ries, car•ried, car•ry•ing**) to take from one place to another. *Will you carry this package home?*

cas•tle /kăs′ əl/ *n.* a large building with high walls, towers, and sometimes a moat. *Kings and queens often live in castles.*

catch¹ /kăch/ *v.* (**catch•es, caught, catch•ing**) **a.** to get; to take and hold onto; to seize. *Watch that boy catch the ball!* **b.** to get to in time. *If you run, you can catch the bus.* **c.** to be held by something. *I always catch my coat on that nail.*

catch² /kăch/ *n.* (**catch•es** *pl.*) a thing that fastens or holds. *The catch on her dress was broken.*

cat•er•pil•lar /kăt′ ər pĭl′ ər/ *n.* the wormlike form, or larva, of a moth or butterfly. *The caterpillar spins a cocoon.*

cav•i•ty /kăv′ ĭ tē/ *n.* (**cav•i•ties** *pl.*) a small hollow caused by decay in a tooth. *If you brush your teeth properly, you won't have many cavities.*

cell /sĕl/ *n.* one of the tiny parts of living matter of which all animals and plants are made. *Some animals and plants are made up of only one cell.*

▶ **Cell** sounds like **sell**.

ce•ment /sĭ mĕnt′/ *n.* a powdered mixture of rock and clay that hardens into concrete when mixed with water. *Cement is used to build sidewalks.*

cent /sĕnt/ *n.* the smallest coin of the United States; a penny. *One hundred cents make a dollar.*

▶ **Cent** sounds like **sent** and **scent**.

cen•ter /sĕn′ tər/ *n.* **a.** a point in the middle. *Stand in the center of the circle.* **b.** a main area or place where people gather. *The town has a new shopping center.*

chain /chān/ *n.* **a.** a number of links or rings fastened together. *She strung the beads on a gold chain.* **b.** a series of things that are connected or joined. *The Rocky Mountains are a chain of mountains.*

chair /châr/ *n.* a piece of furniture with legs and a back that holds one seated person. *Let Grandfather sit in the rocking chair.*

change¹ /chānj/ *v.* (**chang•es, changed, chang•ing**) to make or become different. *She changed her mind.*

change² /chānj/ *n.* **a.** making or becoming different. *Watch for a change in the weather tomorrow.* **b.** small coins. *John has a pocketful of change.*

chase¹ /chās/ *v.* (**chas•es, chased, chas•ing**) **a.** to run after, trying to catch. *The hounds chased the fox.* **b.** to drive away. *She chased the cat away from the bird's nest.*

chase² /chās/ *n.* a chasing. *It was a fine chase, but the fox got away.*

Pronunciation Key

ă	pat	ŏ	pot	th	**th**in
ā	pay	ō	toe	th	**th**is
âr	care	ô	paw, for	hw	**wh**ich
ä	father	oi	noise	zh	vision
ĕ	pet	ou	out	ə	about,
ē	be	o͞o	took		item,
ĭ	pit	o͞o	boot		pencil,
ī	pie	ŭ	cut		gallop,
îr	pier	ûr	urge		circus

check¹ /chĕk/ *v.* to make sure of the correctness of. *Be sure to check your test before you hand it in.*

check² /chĕk/ *n.* **a.** a mark (✓) meaning something is satisfactory. *Make a check if the answer is correct.* **b.** a bill in a restaurant. *The check for our dinners was twelve dollars.* **c.** a written order from a bank to pay money to a certain person or place. *Make out a check for twenty dollars.*

check•up /chĕk′ ŭp′/ *n.* a complete physical examination. *Everyone should have a regular checkup.*

cheese /chēz/ *n.* a food made from the thick part of milk. *I like sandwiches made with cheese.*

cher•ry /chĕr′ ē/ *n.* (**cher•ries** *pl.*) a small, round red or white fruit with a stone or seed in the center. *Some cherries taste sweet, and some taste sour.*

cherry

chew /cho͞o/ *v.* to bite and grind with the teeth. *Chew your food well before you swallow it.*

child /chīld/ *n.* (**chil•dren** *pl.*) **a.** a baby. *The child is just learning to walk.* **b.** a young boy or girl. *Who is the child playing the flute?* **c.** a son or daughter. *I met Mrs. Keefe and her child in the store.*

chil•dren /chĭl′ drən/ plural of **child**.

273

chill•y /chĭl′ē/ adj. cool; somewhat cold. *In the fall the mornings are usually chilly.*

choose /chōōz/ v. (**choos•es, chose, chos•en, choos•ing**) **a.** to pick out. *Choose the kind of candy you want.* **b.** to prefer. *I do not choose to tell you my age.*

chore /chôr/ or /chōr/ n. an odd job; a task around the home. *One of my chores is mowing the lawn.*

church /chûrch/ n. (**church•es** pl.) **a.** a building for public worship. *That church has stained-glass windows.* **b.** a religious service. *Church begins at ten o'clock.*

cir•cle /sûr′kəl/ n. a closed curve that forms a perfectly round figure. *Every part of a circle is the same distance from the center.*

cir•cus /sûr′kəs/ n. (**cir•cus•es** pl.) a show featuring acts with animals, clowns, and acrobats. *A circus may be held under a tent.*

circus

city /sĭt′ē/ n. (**cit•ies** pl.) a large and important town. *Some large cities in the United States are New York, Chicago, Los Angeles, Philadelphia, and Detroit.*

class /klăs/ n. (**class•es** pl.) **a.** a group of students meeting regularly with a teacher. *My English class is the first class of the day.* **b.** persons, animals, or things thought of as a group because they are alike. *Dogs belong to the class of mammals.*

class•room /klăs′rōōm′/ or /klăs′rŏŏm′/ n. a room in a school or college where classes meet. *The children decorated their classroom.*

clerk /klûrk/ n. **a.** a person who works in an office. *A clerk does general office work.* **b.** a person who sells things in a store. *My sister has a summer job as a clerk in a drugstore.*

click¹ /klĭk/ n. a short, sharp sound. *The camera made a click as I pressed the button to take the picture.*

click² /klĭk/ v. to make a short, sharp sound. *The catch clicked shut.*

cliff /klĭf/ n. a high, steep rock with a side that goes almost straight up. *Cliffs are difficult to climb.*

clock /klŏk/ n. a device made for telling time. *Can you see the hands move on that clock?*

close¹ /klōz/ v. (**clos•es, closed, clos•ing**) to shut. *Close the door when you leave.*

close² /klōs/ adj. (**clos•er, clos•est; close•ly**, adv.) near. *We planted the tree close to the house.*

cloth /klôth/ or /klŏth/ n. a material made by weaving threads of cotton, wool, silk, nylon, etc. *Most of our clothes are made of cloth.*

cloud /kloud/ n. a large gray or white mass of tiny water drops floating in the sky. *That big cloud may bring rain.*

cloud•y /klou′dē/ adj. (**cloud•i•er, cloud•i•est; cloud•i•ly**, adv.) full of clouds. *The sky was gray and cloudy.*

clo•ver /klō′vər/ n. a sweet-smelling plant with leaves growing in three parts. *I feed my rabbit clover.*

col•or¹ /kŭl′ər/ n. a hue, tint, or shade caused by the effect of light rays on the eyes. *All colors are combinations of red, yellow, and blue.*

col•or² /kŭl′ər/ v. to change the color. *The children like to color the pictures in their coloring books.*

come /kŭm/ v. (**comes, came, come, com•ing**) **a.** to move toward. *The dark clouds are coming this way.* **b.** to arrive. *What time does the bus come?*

Spelling Dictionary

Pronunciation Key

ă	pat	ŏ	pot	th	**th**in
ā	pay	ō	toe	th	**th**is
âr	care	ô	paw, for	hw	**wh**ich
ä	father	oi	n**oi**se	zh	vi**si**on
ĕ	pet	ou	**ou**t	ə	**a**bout,
ē	be	ŏŏ	took		item,
ĭ	pit	ōō	b**oo**t		pencil,
ī	pie	ŭ	cut		gall**o**p,
îr	pier	ûr	**ur**ge		circ**u**s

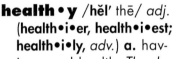

hail¹ /hāl/ *n.* small pieces of ice that may fall during a rainstorm. *Hail makes a noise on the top of a car.*

hail² /hāl/ *v.* to pour down hail. *It is raining and hailing at the same time.*

hair /hâr/ *n.* **a.** the mass of thin, threadlike strands that grow on a person's or an animal's skin. *Elizabeth has beautiful hair; she brushes it often.* **b.** any one of these strands. *Look at the hairs that dog left on the chair!*

▶ **Hair** sounds like **hare**.

hair•cut /hâr′ kŭt′/ *n.* a cutting of the hair. *Tom got a very short haircut from the barber.*

half /hăf/ *n.* (**halves** *pl.*) one of two equal parts. *Which half of the sandwich do you want?*

hap•pen /hăp′ ən/ *v.* to take place; to occur. *Is anything happening tomorrow afternoon?*

hap•py /hăp′ ē/ *adj.* (**hap•pi•er, hap•pi•est; hap•pi•ly,** *adv.*) feeling or showing pleasure; joyful. *The happy man whistled all day.*

hare /hâr/ *n.* an animal like a rabbit, but much larger. *A hare has strong legs and can run fast.*

▶ **Hare** sounds like **hair**.

have /hăv/ *v.* (**has, had, hav•ing**) used as a helping verb in addition to having the following meanings: **a.** to own; to possess. *They have a new house.* **b.** to accept; to take. *Have a piece of pie.* **c.** to be forced; to feel obliged. *I have to do my homework now.*

hawk /hôk/ *n.* a large bird with a strong curved beak, sharp claws, and good eyesight. *A hawk eats smaller birds and animals.*

hawk

health•y /hĕl′ thē/ *adj.* (**health•i•er, health•i•est; health•i•ly,** *adv.*) **a.** having good health. *The doctor said the baby was healthy.* **b.** good for the health. *Broccoli is a healthy food.*

hear /hîr/ *v.* (**hears, heard, hear•ing**) **a.** to take in sound through the ears. *We could hear every word clearly.* **b.** to listen to; to pay attention to. *Did you hear the principal's announcement?*

heard /hŭrd/ past tense of **hear**.

heart /härt/ *n.* **a.** the large hollow muscle that pumps blood throughout the body by contracting and expanding. *The heart keeps the blood in circulation.* **b.** something looking like a heart. *A deck of cards has thirteen cards with hearts on them.*

heat¹ /hēt/ *n.* hotness; great warmth. *Fire gives off heat.*

heat² /hēt/ *v.* to make or become warm. *The furnace heats the house.*

here's /hîrz/ here is.

her•self /hər sĕlf′/ *pron.* **a.** her own self. *Jennifer fell down and hurt herself.* **b.** the person or self she usually is. *Beth isn't acting like herself today.*

he's /hēz/ he is; he has.

hid•den¹ /hǐd′ n/ *adj.* concealed; secret. *The explorers searched for the hidden treasure.*

hid•den² /hǐd′ n/ *v.* a form of **hide.**

hide /hīd/ *v.* (**hides, hid, hid•den, hid•ing**) to put or keep out of sight. *Hide the ribbon somewhere in the room, and we'll try to find it.*

high¹ /hī/ *adj.* **a.** tall; far above the ground. *Walnuts fell from a high branch.* **b.** greater than usual; more than normal. *Prices at this store are high.*

high² /hī/ *n.* a high amount, as in temperature. *Yesterday's high was ninety-eight degrees.*

high•land /hī′ lənd/ *n.* a hilly area that is higher than the land around it. *The shepherd led the flock up to the highland.*

hill•side /hǐl′ sīd′/ *n.* the side of a hill. *In winter we coast down the hillside on our sleds.*

him•self /hǐm sělf′/ *pron.* **a.** his own self. *My little brother tied his shoes all by himself.* **b.** the person or self he usually is. *Jason looked more like himself after the doctor took the cast off his arm.*

hiss¹ /hǐs/ *v.* (**hiss•es, hissed, hiss•ing**) to make a sound like s-s-s-s. *We all love to hiss the villain.*

hiss² /hǐs/ *n.* (**hiss•es** *pl.*) a sound like s-s-s-s. *The goose gave an angry hiss.*

hon•ey /hǔn′ ē/ *n.* a sweet, sticky, yellow liquid made by honeybees. *Honey tastes good on toast.*

hop /hǒp/ *v.* (**hops, hopped, hop•ping**) to move by jumping. *Rabbits hop from place to place.*

hope /hōp/ *v.* (**hopes, hoped, hop•ing**) to expect and desire; to wish. *We hoped Brad would win.*

hop

hot /hǒt/ *adj.* (**hot•ter, hot•test**) **a.** very warm; having a high temperature. *I like taking hot baths.* **b.** sharp to the taste; peppery, spicy. *Do you prefer hot or mild sauce?*

hour•ly¹ /our′ lē/ *adv.* every hour. *The bells in our school ring hourly.*

hour•ly² /our′ lē/ *adj.* for every hour. *She receives an hourly wage of six dollars.*

house /hous/ *n.* a building in which to live. *The fine old house is for sale.*

house•fly /hous′ flī′/ *n.* (**house•flies** *pl.*) a common two-winged flying insect. *There's a housefly in that spiderweb.*

hun•dred /hǔn′ drǐd/ *n.* ten times ten; 100. *Hundreds of children signed up for camp.*

hun•gry /hǔng′ grē/ *adj.* (**hun•gri•er, hun•gri•est; hun•gri•ly,** *adv.*) wanting food; needing food. *The hungry children ate fifty sandwiches.*

hur•ry¹ /hûr′ ē/ or /hǔr′ ē/ *v.* (**hur•ries, hur•ried, hur•ry•ing**) to act quickly; to move fast. *Hurry or you'll be late!*

hur•ry² /hûr′ ē/ or /hǔr′ ē/ *n.* haste; a rush; a fast action. *Why are you in such a hurry?*

hurt /hûrt/ *v.* (**hurts, hurt, hurt•ing**) **a.** to cause pain to. *The sting of the bee hurt his arm.* **b.** to suffer pain. *Does your head hurt?*

I

ice /īs/ *n.* water that has been frozen solid by cold. *Ice keeps food and drinks cool.*

I'll /īl/ I shall; I will.

I'm /īm/ I am.

inch /ǐnch/ *n.* (**inch•es** *pl.*) a measure of length equal to one-twelfth of one foot. *Michelle is forty-six inches tall.*

is•n't /ĭz' ənt/ is not.

its /ĭts/ *pron.* of or belonging to it. *The bird left its nest.*

it's /ĭts/ it is; it has.

jel•ly /jĕl' ē/ *n.* (**jel•lies** *pl.*) a food made by boiling fruit juices and sugar. *I like grape jelly.*

jel•ly•fish /jĕl' ē fĭsh'/ *n.* (**jel•ly•fish** or **jel•ly•fish•es** *pl.*) a soft, bowl-shaped sea animal with an almost transparent body. *Some jellyfish will sting you if you touch them.*

join /join/ *v.* **a.** to put together; to con-nect. *The caboose was joined to the last car of the train.* **b.** to become a member of. *Next year I will be able to join the Boy Scouts.* **c.** to combine with a group in doing something. *Would you like to join our game?*

kind¹ /kīnd/ *adj.* gentle and caring. *They are always very kind to animals.*

kind² /kīnd/ *n.* type; sort; variety. *Which kind of ice cream would you like?*

king•dom /kĭng' dəm/ *n.* a country, land, or territory ruled by a king or queen. *The queen declared a holiday throughout the kingdom.*

kit•ten /kĭt' n/ *n.* a young cat. *The kit-ten chased a butterfly around the garden.*

knew /nōō/ or /nyōō/ past tense of **know.**

knight /nīt/ *n.* during the Middle Ages, a warrior who was honored with a mili-tary rank by a king or lord. *The king called his knights together to plan the battle.*

Pronunciation Key

ă	p**a**t	ŏ	p**o**t	th	**th**in
ā	p**ay**	ō	t**oe**	th	**th**is
âr	c**are**	ô	p**aw**, f**or**	hw	**wh**ich
ä	f**a**ther	oi	n**oi**se	zh	vi**s**ion
ĕ	p**e**t	ou	**ou**t	ə	**a**bout,
ē	b**e**	ŏŏ	t**oo**k		it**e**m,
ĭ	p**i**t	ōō	b**oo**t		penc**i**l,
ī	p**ie**	ŭ	c**u**t		gall**o**p,
îr	p**ier**	ûr	**ur**ge		circ**u**s

know /nō/ *v.* (**knows, knew, known, know•ing**) **a.** to understand; to have information about. *Do you know how fossils are made?* **b.** to be aware; to be sure. *We knew we had heard a noise.* **c.** to be acquainted with. *I've known them for years.* **d.** to have skill in. *Who knows how to play the piano?*

lad•der /lăd' ər/ *n.* a series of steps placed between two long side-pieces, used for climbing. *The painter leaned the ladder against the wall.*

ladder

laid /lād/ past tense of **lay.**

land /lănd/ *n.* **a.** the part of the earth that is not water. *After the plane went up through the clouds, we could no longer see the land.* **b.** ground; earth; soil. *This rich land is good for planting corn.*

large /lärj/ *adj.* (**larg•er, larg•est; large•ly,** *adv.*) big. *A whale is large.*

last /lăst/ *adj.* **a.** coming after all others; final. *The last train leaves at six o'clock.* **b.** before the present time; most recent. *I read this book last year.*

last•ly /lăst' lē/ *adv.* at the end; finally. *Lastly, pour the batter into a cake pan and put it into the oven.*

Spelling Dictionary

late¹ /lāt/ *adj.* (**la•ter, la•test**) **a.** happening after the usual time. *We had a late summer this year.* **b.** near the end of a certain time. *Our tomatoes ripen in late summer.*

late² /lāt/ *adv.* after the usual or proper time. *The bus came late.*

late•ly /lāt' lē/ *adv.* not long ago; recently. *Edna has lately been working harder than ever.*

law /lô/ *n.* a rule. *Every state has a law against stealing.*

lawn /lôn/ *n.* ground covered with grass that is kept cut short. *Mr. Griffin's lawn is smooth and green.*

lawn

lay /lā/ *v.* (**lays, laid, lay•ing**) **a.** to put or place. *You can lay your book on the table.* **b.** to produce eggs. *Hens lay eggs.*

leaf /lēf/ *n.* (**leaves** *pl.*) one of the green, flat parts that grow on bushes, plants, and trees. *The caterpillar was eating a leaf.*

learn /lûrn/ *v.* **a.** to gain skill or knowledge in. *We learn spelling in school.* **b.** to memorize. *Can you learn this poem?* **c.** to find out. *When will we learn the results of the election?*

leave /lēv/ *v.* (**leaves, left, leav•ing**) **a.** to go away; to go from. *The train left ten minutes ago.* **b.** to let stay or be. *Leave your packages here while you shop.*

ledge /lĕj/ *n.* a narrow shelf or ridge, especially on a cliff or rock wall. *We saw an eagle's nest on a ledge high above.*

left¹ /lĕft/ past tense of **leave**.

left² /lĕft/ *adj.* located closer to the side opposite the right. *We took a left turn at the corner.*

left³ /lĕft/ *n.* the left side. *Her house is the one on the left.*

left⁴ /lĕft/ *adv.* in the direction to the left. *Go left after you reach the stoplight.*

less¹ /lĕs/ *adj.* not so much. *It took less time to do my homework this week than last.*

less² /lĕs/ *adv.* to a smaller extent. *I was less happy than I looked.*

les•son /lĕs' ən/ *n.* something to be taught or learned. *My brother is taking violin lessons.*

let•ter /lĕt' ər/ *n.* **a.** a symbol for a sound. *There are twenty-six letters in our alphabet.* **b.** a written or typed message sent by mail. *Mail your letter at the post office.*

lev•er /lĕv' ər/ or /lē' vər/ *n.* a bar used to lift objects. *The lever is rested on a support and pushed at one end to lift the other end.*

lift /lĭft/ *v.* to raise from a lower to a higher position. *This box is too heavy for me to lift.*

light¹ /līt/ *n.* **a.** rays of energy that help us see; the opposite of dark. *The sun gives light.* **b.** anything that gives light. *Turn off the light when you leave the room.*

light² /līt/ *adj.* not heavy; not having much weight. *In the summer we wear light clothes.*

line /līn/ *n.* **a.** a rope, cord, or wire. *Fishing line must be strong.* **b.** a long, thin mark. *Draw a line on your paper.* **c.** a row of persons or things. *There was a long line at the movie theater.*

lip /lĭp/ *n.* either of the two edges of the mouth. *Your lips move when you speak.*

list¹ /lĭst/ *n.* a column of names, words, or numbers. *Please write "milk" on the grocery list.*

list² /lĭst/ *v.* to write or print in a column or columns. *List the spelling words on your paper.*

lit•er /lē′ tər/ n. a metric unit of volume used to measure both liquids and dry matter. *A liter of milk is about the same as a quart of milk.*

lit•tle[1] /lĭt′ l/ adj. **a.** small. *An elephant is big and an ant is little.* **b.** not much. *There is little food in the house.*

lit•tle[2] /lĭt′ l/ n. a small amount. *Patricia showed the teacher a little of her poetry.*

live /lĭv/ v. (**lives, lived, liv•ing**) **a.** to be alive; to exist. *We live on the planet Earth.* **b.** to have one's home; to dwell. *Our aunt lives in Texas.*

liv•ing /lĭv′ ĭng/ adj. alive; not dead. *Biology is the study of living things.*

load[1] /lōd/ n. something that is carried. *The load was too heavy for the small car.*

load[2] /lōd/ v. to fill with something to be carried. *Load the truck with bricks.*

log•ging /lô′ gĭng/ or /lŏg′ ĭng/ n. the work of cutting down trees and making them into logs. *Logging is a big industry.*

loose /loōs/ adj. (**loos•er, loos•est; loose•ly,** adv.) not fastened tightly. *The bottom step is loose.*

lose /loōz/ v. (**los•es, lost, los•ing**) **a.** to be unable to find. *Don't lose your key.* **b.** to fail to win. *Our team almost lost the game.*

lost[1] /lôst/ or /lŏst/ v. past tense of **lose.**

lost[2] /lôst/ or /lŏst/ adj. **a.** missing. *The children found the lost cat.* **b.** destroyed; ruined. *The lost trees will take years to replace.*

loud /loud/ adj. **a.** strong in sound; not soft or quiet. *My alarm clock is loud.* **b.** noisy. *The people in the next apartment have loud parties.*

love[1] /lŭv/ n. **a.** a deep, fond, affectionate feeling. *Helping people is a way of showing love.* **b.** a great liking. *He has a love of books.*

Pronunciation Key

ă	pat	ŏ	pot	th	**th**in
ā	pay	ō	toe	th	**th**is
âr	care	ô	paw, for	hw	**wh**ich
ä	father	oi	noise	zh	vision
ĕ	pet	ou	out	ə	about,
ē	be	oŏ	took		item,
ĭ	pit	oō	boot		pencil,
ī	pie	ŭ	cut		gallop,
îr	pier	ûr	urge		circus

love[2] /lŭv/ v. (**loves, loved, lov•ing**) **a.** to have a deep affection for. *My parents love me.* **b.** to like very much. *Emily loves to play soccer.*

low•land /lō′ lənd/ n. an area that is lower and flatter than the land around it. *A marsh is often a lowland.*

lunch /lŭnch/ n. (**lunch•es** pl.) a light meal eaten around the middle of the day. *We have lunch at noon.*

M

ma•chine /mə shēn′/ n. **a.** a device for doing work. *Levers, pulleys, and wheels are simple machines.* **b.** a combination of parts, both moving and fixed, for doing work. *Do you know how to use a sewing machine?*

mail[1] /māl/ n. packages, letters, postcards, etc., that are delivered through the post office. *Has the mail come yet?*

mail

mail[2] /māl/ v. to send by mail; to place in a mailbox. *Did you mail my letter?*

main /mān/ adj. most important; chief; major. *Roast beef was the main course.*

main•ly /mān′ lē/ adv. for the most part; chiefly. *The book was mainly about history.*

Spelling Dictionary

make /māk/ v. (makes, made, mak•ing) **a.** to put together; to build; to create. *Let's make a tent out of blankets.* **b.** to cause; to bring about. *A horn makes a loud noise.* **c.** to equal; to add up to. *Two and three make five.*

ma•ple /mā′ pəl/ n. a tree with hard wood and a thin sap that is sometimes used in making syrup and sugar. *Maples are grown for both beauty and shade.*

math /măth/ n. the study of numbers and their relations to each other; mathematics. *We learned the times tables in math.*

may•be /mā′ bē/ adv. perhaps. *Maybe he hasn't left the train yet, and we can still find him.*

meal /mēl/ n. the food eaten at one time. *We had a big meal on Thanksgiving.*

meal

mean¹ /mēn/ v. (means, meant, mean•ing) **a.** to indicate the idea of. *What does this word mean?* **b.** to have in mind as a purpose. *She didn't mean to get angry.*

mean² /mēn/ adj. unkind; wicked. *The man was mean to the children who walked on his lawn.*

meas•ure¹ /mĕzh′ ər/ n. a unit used in finding the length, size, or amount of something. *A mile, a pound, and a quart are common measures.*

meas•ure² /mĕzh′ ər/ v. (meas•ures, meas•ured, meas•ur•ing) to find the length, size, or amount of something. *They measured the floor for the new carpet.*

meat /mēt/ n. the flesh of an animal used as food. *Lean meat is better for you.*

med•i•cine /mĕd′ ĭ sĭn/ n. anything used to cure or prevent disease or improve health. *The doctor gave me some medicine to take.*

mer•ry /mĕr′ ē/ adj. (mer•ri•er, mer•ri•est; mer•ri•ly, adv.) full of happiness and cheer; joyful. *There was a merry crowd at the football game.*

me•ter /mē′ tər/ n. a unit of length in the metric system. *A meter is about thirty-nine inches.*

met•ric /mĕt′ rĭk/ adj. of or using the metric system. *Metric measurement is used in scientific experiments.*

mice /mīs/ plural of **mouse.**

mild /mīld/ adj. **a.** not harsh; not severe; warm rather than cold. *We had a mild winter last year.* **b.** not sharp or biting to the taste. *We ordered mild sauce on our food.*

mill /mĭl/ n. **a.** a building with machinery in which something is manufactured. *Cloth is made in a textile mill.* **b.** a building in which grain is ground into flour. *The farmers brought their wheat to the mill.*

mine¹ /mīn/ n. a large hole, pit, or tunnel in the earth from which minerals can be taken. *We visited a coal mine in West Virginia.*

mine² /mīn/ v. (mines, mined, min•ing) to dig mines to locate and remove minerals. *The workers are mining coal.*

mi•nus¹ /mī′ nəs/ prep. less. *Eleven minus two is nine.*

mi•nus² /mī′ nəs/ n. (mi•nus•es pl.) a sign (−) that shows that the number following it is to be subtracted. *Did you notice the minus before the second number?*

Miss /mĭs/ n. title used before an unmarried woman's last name. *When Miss Hansen got married, she became Mrs. Moore.*

mit•ten /mĭt′ n/ n. a glove worn in winter with a single covering for the fingers and a separate covering for the thumb. *Mittens keep our fingers warm.*

mon•ey /mŭn′ ē/ *n.*
any metal or paper
that is issued for use in
buying and selling. *Do
you have any money
in your pocket?*

money

month /mŭnth/ *n.* one
of the twelve parts into which a year is
divided. *The first month is January.*

month•ly¹ /mŭnth′ lē/ *adj.* happening
once a month. *Did you pay the monthly
bills?*

month•ly² /mŭnth′ lē/ *adv.* once
each month. *This magazine is published
monthly.*

moon•light /mōon′ līt/ *n.* the light of
the moon. *The moonlight helped the trav-
elers find their way in the night.*

morn•ing /môr′ nĭng/ *n.* the earliest
part of the day, ending at noon. *We eat
breakfast every morning.*

most /mōst/ *adj.* greatest in amount,
number, etc. *The team from Atlanta
scored the most points.*

moth•er /mŭth′ ər/ *n.* the female parent. *The teacher wants to see my father
and mother.*

mouse /mous/ *n.* (**mice** *pl.*) a small animal with white, gray, or brown fur, a
long tail, and long, sharp front teeth.
Field mice make nests in the ground.

Mr. /mĭs′ tər/ *n.* a title used before a
man's last name. *Mr. Williams is our new
neighbor.*

Mrs. /mĭs′ iz/ *n.* a title used before a
married woman's last name. *Our
teacher's name is Mrs. Sloane.*

Ms. /mĭz/ *n.* a title used before a
woman's last name. *Ms. Velazquez is the
president of our bank.*

mud•dy /mŭd′ ē/ *adj.* (**mud•di•er,
mud•di•est**) covered with mud. *Take
your muddy shoes off before you come
inside.*

mul•ti•ply /mŭl′ tə plī/ *v.*
(**mul•ti•plies, mul•ti•plied,
mul•ti•ply•ing**) to add the same number
to itself a certain number of times. *When
12 is multiplied by 3, it is the same as
adding 12 + 12 + 12.*

nerve /nûrv/ *n.* one of the fibers that
carry messages and feelings between
the brain and the rest of the body.
*Nerves in the skin allow us to feel heat
and cold.*

nest¹ /nĕst/ *n.* **a.** a place built by a
bird for laying eggs. *The robin built its
nest outside my window.* **b.** a place
where insects or animals live. *Wasps
build nests.*

nest² /nĕst/ *v.* to build and use a nest.
Birds nest in trees.

nev•er /nĕv′ ər/ *adv.* not ever; not at
any time. *Maria has never been late to
school; she is always early.*

news /nōoz/ or /nyōoz/ *n.* **a.** information; things that a person has not heard
about. *What is the news about your
brother's new job?* **b.** recent happenings
reported in newspapers and over television and radio. *We read the news in
the paper.*

Spelling Dictionary

nick•el /nĭk′ əl/ n. a small coin worth five cents. *A nickel is bigger than a penny.*

night /nīt/ n. the time between evening and morning; the time from sunset to sunrise when it is dark. *The stars shine at night.*

no•bod•y /nō′ bŏd′ ē/ or /nō′ bə dē/ pron. no one; no person. *Nobody is here at this time of day.*

none /nŭn/ pron. not any; not one. *None of us had the bus fare, so we walked.*

north¹ /nôrth/ n. the direction to your right when you face the sunset. *Cold winds blow from the north.*

north² /nôrth/ adj. to the north. *The north side of the house faces the highway.*

north³ /nôrth/ adv. toward the north. *Birds fly north in the spring.*

noth•ing /nŭth′ ĭng/ n. **a.** not anything. *We saw nothing we liked in that shop.* **b.** zero. *Six taken from six leaves nothing.*

num•ber /nŭm′ bər/ n. **a.** the count or total sum of persons or things; the amount. *What is the number of students in your class?* **b.** a word or figure that tells how many. *Four is my favorite number.*

oak /ōk/ n. a large tree having hard wood and nuts called acorns. *That tall tree is an oak.*

o•cean /ō′ shən/ n. **a.** the large body of salt water that covers much of the earth's surface; the sea. *Ships sail on the ocean.* **b.** any of its five main divisions—Atlantic, Pacific, Indian, Arctic, or Antarctic. *Which ocean is the largest?*

oc•to•pus /ŏk′ tə pəs/ n. (**oc•to•pus•es** or **oc•to•pi** pl.) a sea animal having a soft body and eight arms called tentacles. *An octopus uses its arms to grasp things.*

odd /ŏd/ adj. **a.** strange; not usual. *What an odd thing to say!* **b.** not able to be divided evenly by the number two. *The smallest odd numbers are 1 and 3.*

oh /ō/ interj. a sound that expresses surprise, interest, or sorrow. *Oh, no! I forgot my keys!*

oil /oil/ n. a greasy liquid obtained from animals, plants, or minerals. *Please put oil on the rusty wheel.*

oil

once /wŭns/ adv. **a.** one time. *We met only once.* **b.** formerly. *Horses once were used to plow fields.*

o•pen¹ /ō′ pən/ v. **a.** to move from a shut position. *Open the door.* **b.** to remove the outer cover. *Open the envelope.*

o•pen² /ō′ pən/ adj. not closed or shut. *The cat climbed out an open window.*

or•der /ôr′ dər/ n. **a.** a command; an instruction. *The sailors obeyed the captain's orders.* **b.** the way in which things follow one another. *These names are in alphabetical order.*

or•gan /ôr′ gən/ n. **a.** a keyboard instrument that makes music by sending air through a set of pipes. *Who played the organ at the wedding?* **b.** a part of an animal or plant that has a special duty. *The eyes, heart, and stomach are organs.*

oth•er¹ /ŭth′ ər/ adj. **a.** different. *I asked the salesman to call some other day.* **b.** remaining. *Can you write with your other hand?*

oth•er² /ŭth′ ər/ pron. the remaining one; the other one. *Raise one hand, and then raise the other.*

Spelling Dictionary

o•ver¹ /ō′ vər/ *prep.* **a.** above. *The reading lamp is over the bed.* **b.** on top of. *Put the cover over the basket.* **c.** more than. *The flight took over three hours.*

o•ver² /ō′ vər/ *adv.* again. *Do this exercise over.*

o•ver³ /ō′ vər/ *adj.* ended. *The rain is over.*

owe /ō/ *v.* (**owes, owed, ow•ing**) to have to pay or repay in return for something. *Brad owes Jon a dollar.*

owl /oul/ *n.* a bird with a large head, large eyes, and sharp claws. *Owls fly mostly at night.*

pace /pās/ *v.* (**pac•es, paced, pac•ing**) to walk with regular steps. *The leopard paced in its cage.*

page /pāj/ *n.* one side of a sheet of paper in a book, magazine, newspaper, or letter. *Kurt knew from the first page that he would like the book.*

paid /pād/ past tense of **pay.**

pail /pāl/ *n.* a round bucket with a handle. *We filled the pails with water.*

pain /pān/ *n.* an ache, hurt, or sore feeling. *The pain in Robin's arm soon went away.*

paint¹ /pānt/ *n.* a mixture used to color a surface. *Where's the jar of blue paint?*

paint

paint² /pānt/ *v.* **a.** to cover a surface with paint. *They painted the fence.* **b.** to make a picture with paints. *Ms. Lindquist paints landscapes in her spare time.*

pair /pâr/ *n.* **a.** two things of the same kind that go together; a set of two. *Carlos has a new pair of shoes.* **b.** a couple. *A pair of robins built their nest in a tree.*

▶ **Pair** sounds like **pear.**

Pronunciation Key

ă	pat	ŏ	pot	th	thin
ā	pay	ō	toe	th	this
âr	care	ô	paw, for	hw	which
ä	father	oi	noise	zh	vision
ĕ	pet	ou	out	ə	about,
ē	be	ŏŏ	took		item,
ĭ	pit	ōō	boot		pencil,
ī	pie	ŭ	cut		gallop,
îr	pier	ûr	urge		circus

part•ly /pärt′ lē/ *adv.* in part; not completely. *My test is partly finished.*

pave /pāv/ *v.* (**paves, paved, pav•ing**) to cover a road, street, etc., with a smooth, hard surface. *The dirt road will be paved next week.*

pay /pā/ *v.* (**pays, paid, pay•ing**) to give money to someone for goods or for something done. *Kim paid three dollars for her lunch.*

peace /pēs/ *n.* **a.** quiet and calm; stillness. *We like the peace of the country.* **b.** freedom from war. *Every thinking person wants peace.*

peak /pēk/ *n.* **a.** the pointed top of a mountain. *We hiked up to a snowy peak.* **b.** the highest point. *It rained hardest during the storm's peak.*

pear /pâr/ *n.* a juicy fruit with a mild flavor. *A pear is usually larger at the bottom end.*

▶ **Pear** sounds like **pair.**

pen•cil /pĕn′ səl/ *n.* a long, slender piece of wood with a center of black or colored writing material. *Pencils are used for writing and for drawing.*

peo•ple /pē′ pəl/ *n.* human beings; persons; men, women, boys, and girls. *People of all ages attended the fair.*

pep•per /pĕp′ ər/ *n.* a hot-tasting powdered spice. *Pepper is used to season foods.*

pic•to•graph /pĭk′ tə grăf′/ *n.* a diagram or chart that uses pictures to stand for words or numbers. *This pictograph shows the number of students in each class.*

pie /pī/ *n.* a baked food made of fruit, meat, or pudding within a crust. *Apple pie is his favorite food.*

pi•lot /pī′ lət/ *n.* a person who flies an airplane. *Airline pilots must have years of training.*

pint /pīnt/ *n.* a measure of volume equal to one half of a quart. *We bought a pint of cream.*

place¹ /plās/ *n.* **a.** a certain point; a spot. *The coolest place in town is near the river.* **b.** a space where something belongs. *Put the chair back in its place.* **c.** a seat or space for a person. *If you get there early, save me a place.*

place² /plās/ *v.* (**plac•es, placed, plac•ing**) to put in a particular position; to set. *Place your pencil on the desk.*

plain /plān/ *adj.* (**plain•ly,** *adv.*) **a.** easy to see; clear. *The directions are plain.* **b.** simple; not fancy in appearance. *Tracy wore a plain blue dress.*
▶ **Plain** sounds like **plane.**

plan¹ /plăn/ *n.* a way of doing something that is thought out in advance; a scheme. *Mark is excited about his plan for a vacation in California.*

plan² /plăn/ *v.* (**plans, planned, plan•ning**) to think out in advance. *Amy helped us plan the bake sale.*

plane /plān/ *n.* an airplane. *The big planes take off from the airport one minute apart.*
▶ **Plane** sounds like **plain.**

play•ground /plā′ ground′/ *n.* a place for playing, used by children. *Swings and slides are in the playground.*

plot /plŏt/ *n.* a small section of ground. *Kevin and Jason each has his own plot.*

plus¹ /plŭs/ *prep.* added to; and. *Four plus two is six.*

plus² /plŭs/ *n.* (**plus•es** *pl.*) a sign (**+**) that shows that the number following it is to be added. *Is that a plus or a minus?*

point¹ /point/ *n.* **a.** a sharp end. *I like a pencil with a fine point.* **b.** a position; a place. *We are at this point on the map.* **c.** a unit of scoring. *She won the game by two points.*

point

point² /point/ *v.* to aim. *He pointed his arrow at the target.*

pool /pool/ *n.* a tank filled with water and used for swimming. *Peter swam across the pool.*

pound /pound/ *n.* a measure of weight equal to sixteen ounces. *Buy a pound of flour for me.*

pres•i•dent /prĕz′ ĭ dənt/ *n.* the person who occupies the highest office in a nation, business, club, college, etc. *Lisa is president of the nature club.*

pret•ty /prĭt′ ē/ *adj.* (**pret•ti•er, pret•ti•est; pret•ti•ly,** *adv.*) lovely; pleasing; pleasant to look at or to hear. *The garden was filled with pretty flowers.*

price /prīs/ *n.* the cost in money; the amount of money for which something is sold. *The price should be clearly labeled.*

prince /prĭns/ *n.* the son of a king or queen. *The prince in the story rode a white horse.*

prin•cess /prĭn′ sĭs/ or /prĭn′ sĕs′/ *n.* (**prin•cess•es** *pl.*) the daughter of a king or queen. *A princess sometimes wears a crown.*

prize /prīz/ *n.* a thing won in a contest. *Tony won the prize for spelling the most words correctly.*

proud /proud/ *adj.* **a.** having a proper regard for oneself. *Mr. Collins is a proud man who likes to do his job well.* **b.** having satisfaction and pleasure. *The proud mother watched her daughter graduate.*

pue•blo /pwĕb′ lō/ *n.* a flat-roofed village of the Southwest built of adobe and stone. *We watched a woman weaving outside the pueblo.*

pul•ley /pŏŏl′ ē/ *n.* a wheel with a furrow in the rim through which a rope moves, used to run a machine or lift a heavy object. *The men used a pulley to lift the big piano onto the truck.*

pup•py /pŭp′ ē/ *n.* (**pup•pies** *pl.*) a young dog; a pup. *The silly puppy tried to chase its own tail.*

put /pŏŏt/ *v.* (**puts, put, put•ting**) **a.** to place; to set. *Put the books on the desk.* **b.** to bring into a certain state. *Put the room in order.*

rab•bit /răb′ ĭt/ *n.* a small, swift animal with long ears, soft fur, and a short tail. *Rabbits live in holes.*

rac•coon /ră kŏŏn′/ *n.* a small animal having gray fur, a bushy tail, and a mark on its face that looks like a black mask. *Raccoons live in trees.*

raccoon

rain•bow /rān′ bō′/ *n.* a curved band of colored light in the sky, caused by the rays of the sun passing through drops of rain, mist, or spray. *We saw a rainbow where the waves broke against the rocks.*

raise /rāz/ *v.* (**rais•es, raised, rais•ing**) **a.** to put up; to lift. *Raise the window for more air.* **b.** to grow. *They raise oranges on that farm.*

Pronunciation Key

ă	pat	ŏ	pot	th	**th**in
ā	pay	ō	toe	th	**th**is
âr	care	ô	paw, for	hw	**wh**ich
ä	father	oi	n**oi**se	zh	vi**s**ion
ĕ	pet	ou	**ou**t	ə	**a**bout,
ē	be	ŏŏ	t**oo**k		item,
ĭ	pit	ōō	b**oo**t		penc**i**l,
ī	pie	ŭ	c**u**t		gall**o**p,
îr	p**ier**	ûr	**ur**ge		circ**u**s

raw /rô/ *adj.* not cooked. *Strawberries and radishes can be eaten raw.*

real /rē′ əl/ or /rēl/ *adj.* **a.** actual; true; not imagined; not made up. *My uncle told us a real story about his trip to Brazil.* **b.** genuine. *Her necklace is made of real pearls.*

re•al•ly /rē′ ə lē/ or /rē′ lē/ *adv.* truly; in fact. *Nancy can really run fast.*

red /rĕd/ *adj.* (**red•der, red•dest**) a bright color like that of a ruby or a strawberry. *Stop signs are always red.*

re•group /rē grŏŏp′/ *v.* to arrange differently; to put into a new grouping. *You must sometimes regroup numbers before you can subtract.*

re•name /rē nām′/ *v.* (**re•names, re•named, re•nam•ing**) to call by a different name; give a new name to. *We can rename one ten as ten ones.*

re•source /rĭ sôrs′/ or /rē′ sôrs′/ *n.* **a.** an available supply of something that can bring wealth. *Oil is a natural resource.* **b.** anything that can be put to use. *Helping hands are our greatest resource.*

rib•bon /rĭb′ ən/ *n.* a narrow strip of fabric, especially one used as a decoration. *She wore a yellow ribbon in her hair.*

right[1] /rīt/ *adj.* **a.** just; good. *Obeying the law is the right thing to do.* **b.** correct; true; accurate. *Allan's answers were all right.* **c.** located on the side opposite to left. *Raise your right hand.*

right² /rīt/ *adv.* **a.** correctly; accurately. *Do your work right.* **b.** straight on; directly. *He looked right at me.* **c.** to the right side. *Turn right at the second stop light.*

▶ **Right** sounds like **write**.

rob•in /rŏb′ ĭn/ *n.* a bird with a reddish breast and a dark back. *We saw a robin on the lawn.*

robin

roof /rōōf/ or /rŏŏf/ *n.* **a.** the part that covers the top of a house or building. *Many houses have sloping roofs.* **b.** anything like a roof. *The peanut butter stuck to the roof of her mouth.*

root /rōōt/ or /rŏŏt/ *n.* the part of a plant that grows beneath the ground. *Many weeds have strong roots.*

round /round/ *adj.* **a.** shaped like a ball. *The earth is round.* **b.** shaped like a circle. *Our swimming pool is square, but theirs is round.*

row¹ /rō/ *n.* a line formed by a number of persons or things. *Who is sitting in the last row?*

row² /rō/ *v.* to move a boat by using oars. *He rowed across the lake and back.*

rub /rŭb/ *v.* (**rubs, rubbed, rub•bing**) to move something back and forth against another surface. *We had to rub hard to get all the dirt off.*

run /rŭn/ *v.* (**runs, ran, run, run•ning**) **a.** to move by lifting the legs quickly off the ground one after the other. *Teresa ran to second base.* **b.** to go along a certain path. *The road runs past the lake.* **c.** to flow. *Water runs downhill.*

rush¹ /rŭsh/ *v.* (**rush•es, rushed, rush•ing**) to move quickly, often with force. *The wind rushed past the windows.*

rush² /rŭsh/ *n.* an excited state of activity; hurry. *Jill was in a rush to get to school on time.*

sad /săd/ *adj.* (**sad•der, sad•dest; sad•ly,** *adv.*) **a.** unhappy. *We were sad when our team lost.* **b.** causing unhappiness. *Do you cry when you read a sad book?*

safe•ty /sāf′ tē/ *n.* freedom from injury or danger. *Police officers care about your safety.*

sail¹ /sāl/ *n.* a large sheet of heavy cloth used to move a boat through water by catching the wind. *The largest ships used to have thirty sails.*

sail² /sāl/ *v.* to move swiftly, especially in air or on water. *The ship sailed down the river.*

▶ **Sail** sounds like **sale**.

sale /sāl/ *n.* **a.** the selling of something; an exchanging of goods for money. *How much money would the sale of the house bring?* **b.** a special selling at prices lower than usual. *The store was crowded during the sale.*

▶ **Sale** sounds like **sail**.

sand /sănd/ *n.* tiny bits of stone in large amounts, found in the deserts and on shores along oceans, lakes, and rivers. *This beach has smooth sand.*

sang /săng/ past tense of **sing**.

scent /sĕnt/ *n.* an odor; a smell. *The dogs followed the scent of the fox.*

▶ **Scent** sounds like **cent** and **sent**.

school /skōōl/ *n.* **a.** a place for teaching and learning. *Children learn how to read in school.* **b.** the regular time when teaching and learning take place. *We had no school because of the storm.*

score /skôr/ or /skōr/ *n.* **a.** the number of points made in a game. *The final score in the baseball game was 5 to 0.* **b.** a grade. *His score on the test was 93.*

scratch¹ /skrăch/ *v.* **a.** to mark or cut slightly. *Set the box down gently so you won't scratch the tabletop.* **b.** to rub or scrape with the fingers or nails. *Never scratch a mosquito bite.*

scratch² /skrăch/ *n.* (**scratch•es** *pl.*) a slight mark or cut. *A diamond can leave a scratch on glass.*

scrib • ble /skrĭb′ əl/ *v.* (**scrib•bles, scrib•bled, scrib•bling**) to write carelessly and in a hurry. *I barely had time to scribble a letter home last night.*

scrub /skrŭb′/ *v.* (**scrubs, scrubbed, scrub•bing**) to wash or clean by rubbing hard. *At camp we had to scrub and mop the floors.*

sea horse /sē′ hôrs′/ *n.* a kind of small fish with a curling tail and a head that looks like a horse's head. *The sea horse lives in warm seas around the world.*

seed • ling /sēd′ lĭng/ *n.* a young plant or tree that has grown from a seed. *We plant our tomato seedlings in the spring.*

seg • ment /sĕg′ mənt/ *n.* any one of the parts into which a thing is divided. *The line segment extended from point A to point B.*

sell /sĕl/ *v.* (**sells, sold, sell•ing**) **a.** to exchange for money or other payment. *Matt sold his old radio for five dollars.* **b.** to keep for sale; to deal in. *A bakery sells bread, rolls, cookies, and cakes.*
► **Sell** sounds like **cell.**

send /sĕnd/ *v.* (**sends, sent, send•ing**) to cause or order to go. *The principal sent the children home early because of the storm.*

sent /sĕnt/ past tense of **send.**
► **Sent** sounds like **cent** and **scent.**

Pronunciation Key

ă	pat	ŏ	pot	th	**th**in
ā	pay	ō	toe	th	**th**is
âr	care	ô	paw, for	hw	**wh**ich
ä	father	oi	noise	zh	vi**s**ion
ĕ	pet	ou	**ou**t	ə	**a**bout,
ē	be	ŏŏ	took		item,
ĭ	pit	ōō	boot		penc**i**l
ī	pie	ŭ	cut		gall**o**p,
îr	pier	ûr	**ur**ge		circ**u**s

sev • en • teen /sĕv′ ən tēn′/ *n.* the next number after sixteen; ten plus seven; 17. *Some students finish high school at age seventeen.*

sev • enth¹ /sĕv′ ənth/ *adj.* coming next after the sixth. *The seventh day of the week is Saturday.*

sev • enth² /sĕv′ ənth/ *n.* one of seven equal parts. *Since there were seven of us, we divided the pizza into sevenths.*

sew /sō/ *v.* (**sews, sewed, sewn, sew•ing**) to fasten with stitches made by a needle and thread. *He is sewing the buttons on the coat.*

shall /shăl/ *v.* (**should**) **a.** am, is, or are going to. *I shall be there tomorrow.* **b.** must; am, is, or are obliged to. *You shall do your duty.*

shake /shāk/ *v.* (**shakes, shook, shak•en, shak•ing**) to move quickly up and down or from side to side. *Shake the can of orange juice before you open it.*

shape /shāp/ *n.* **a.** form; appearance. *The shape of an apple is round.* **b.** condition. *Regular exercise will keep you in good shape.*

shark /shärk/ *n.* a large ocean fish that eats other fish. *A shark has strong, sharp teeth.*

shark

sharp /shärp/ *adj.* (**sharp•er, sharp•est; sharp•ly,** *adv.*) **a.** having a fine point or a thin edge for cutting. *The knife blade is sharp.* **b.** abrupt; sudden; not gradual. *Slow down the car for the sharp turn just ahead.*

she's /shēz/ she is; she has.

sheep /shēp/ *n.* (**sheep** *pl.*) a hoofed animal with a thick, woolly coat. *Farmers raise sheep both for meat and for wool.*

ship•ping /shĭp' ĭng/ *n.* the action or business of sending goods by ship, truck, train, or air. *Shipping is a major industry.*

shirt /shûrt/ *n.* a garment for the upper part of the body. *Most shirts have a collar and sleeves.*

shirt

shook /shook/ past tense of **shake.**

shoot /shoot/ *v.* (**shoots, shot, shoot•ing**) **a.** to fire a gun. *Mrs. Hill will shoot a pistol to start the race.* **b.** to send out swiftly. *The archer shot an arrow at the target.*

shore•line /shôr' līn'/ or /shōr' līn'/ *n.* the line where the water meets the land. *We watched the surf along the shoreline.*

short•ly /shôrt' lē/ *adv.* in a short time; soon. *We will go home shortly.*

shot[1] /shŏt/ past tense of **shoot.**

shot[2] /shŏt/ *n.* an injection through a needle. *Children get shots to prevent measles and polio.*

should /shood/ *v.* **a.** have a duty to; ought to. *I should study tonight.* **b.** expect to. *We should be able to come.* **c.** past tense of **shall.**

side /sīd/ *n.* **a.** a surface or a line that forms the edge of something. *A triangle has three sides.* **b.** a place or direction. *It's on the other side of town.*

side•walk /sīd' wôk'/ *n.* a path for walking at the side of a street. *Let's skate on the sidewalk.*

sigh[1] /sī/ *v.* to let out a long, deep breath. *When Todd won, he sighed with relief.*

sigh[2] /sī/ *n.* the act of sighing. *She gave a sigh of sadness.*

sight /sīt/ *n.* **a.** the power or ability to see. *A pilot's sight must be good.* **b.** something that is seen. *The sunset last night was a lovely sight.*

sign /sīn/ *n.* **a.** something that stands for something else; a symbol. *The sign for adding is "+."* **b.** a board or space used for advertising or for information. *The traffic sign says "No Parking."*

sig•nal[1] /sĭg' nəl/ *n.* a sign or movement that gives notice of something. *A red traffic light is a signal for "stop."*

sig•nal[2] /sĭg' nəl/ *v.* to tell by using a signal. *The policewoman signaled the driver to stop.*

since[1] /sĭns/ *conj.* **a.** because. *Since I bought a new catcher's mitt, I'd like to give you the old one.* **b.** after the time that. *I haven't seen him since he moved away.*

since[2] /sĭns/ *prep.* ever after. *We've lived here since 1997.*

sing /sĭng/ *v.* (**sings, sang, sung, sing•ing**) **a.** to make music with the voice. *Molly likes to sing in the shower.* **b.** to perform or present in song. *Mr. Cortez sang a solo at the concert.* **c.** to make pleasant whistling sounds. *Birds sing.*

sis•ter /sĭs' tər/ *n.* a girl or woman having the same parents as another person. *Steve has two sisters.*

sit /sĭt/ *v.* (**sits, sat, sit•ting**) to rest on the lower part of the body. *Dad always sits in this chair.*

six•teen /sĭks' tēn'/ *n.* the next number after fifteen; ten plus six; 16. *You can get your driver's license when you are sixteen.*

sixth¹ /sĭksth/ *adj.* coming next after the fifth. *The sixth boy in line is my brother.*

sixth² /sĭksth/ *n.* one of six equal parts. *How can I divide this into sixths?*

six•ty-one /sĭks′ tē wŭn′/ *n.* the next number after sixty; sixty plus one; 61. *He will retire when he is sixty-one.*

size /sīz/ *n.* **a.** the amount of space that a thing takes up. *Look at the size of that elephant!* **b.** one of a series of measures. *Which size paintbrush do you need?*

skate¹ /skāt/ *n.* **a.** a shoe with a blade for moving over ice. *If the pond is frozen, we can use our skates.* **b.** a shoe with four wheels; a roller skate. *You can rent skates at the arena.*

skate² /skāt/ *v.* (**skates, skat•ed, skat•ing**) to move along on skates. *Don't skate so fast.*

sketch /skĕch/ *n.* (**sketch•es** *pl.*) a simple, rough drawing that is made quickly. *The artist drew sketches of the people in the park.*

skirt /skûrt/ *n.* **a.** the part of a dress that hangs below the waist. *She wore a dress with a long skirt.* **b.** a garment that hangs from the waist. *Many girls wear sweaters and skirts in the fall.*

skunk /skŭngk/ *n.* a small animal with a bushy tail and dark fur that has a white stripe down the middle of its back. *A skunk can give off a bad smell.*

skunk

sled¹ /slĕd/ *n.* a low platform on runners that slides over ice and snow. *It is fun to coast down a hill on a sled.*

sled² /slĕd/ *v.* (**sleds, sled•ded, sled•ding**) to travel on a sled. *We went sledding after the first snowfall.*

sleep¹ /slēp/ *v.* (**sleeps, slept, sleep•ing**) to rest the body and the mind by closing the eyes and losing awareness. *Did you sleep through the movie?*

Pronunciation Key

ă	pat	ŏ	pot	th	thin
ā	pay	ō	toe	th	this
âr	care	ô	paw, for	hw	which
ä	father	oi	noise	zh	vision
ĕ	pet	ou	out	ə	about,
ē	be	ŏŏ	took		item,
ĭ	pit	ōō	boot		pencil,
ī	pie	ŭ	cut		gallop,
îr	pier	ûr	urge		circus

sleep² /slēp/ *n.* a state of rest; not being awake. *Most people need at least eight hours of sleep each night.*

slept /slĕpt/ past tense of **sleep**.

slice¹ /slīs/ *n.* a thin, flat piece cut from something. *Give everyone a slice of bread.*

slice² /slīs/ *v.* (**slic•es, sliced, slic•ing**) to cut into slices. *Mom sliced the watermelon.*

slid /slĭd/ past tense of **slide**.

slide¹ /slīd/ *v.* (**slides, slid, slid•ing**) to move smoothly and easily over a surface. *The skier slid over the snow.*

slide² /slīd/ *n.* a smooth surface on which a person can slide. *Children like to go down the slide at the playground.*

slow /slō/ *adj.* (**slow•ly**, *adv.*) **a.** not fast or quick. *The turtle makes slow but steady progress.* **b.** behind time. *Your watch is slow.*

smile¹ /smīl/ *v.* (**smiles, smiled, smil•ing**) to look happy or amused by turning up the mouth at the corners. *The teachers smiled as we sang our songs.*

smile² /smīl/ *n.* the act of smiling; a smiling expression. *A smile can make your day brighter.*

smoke¹ /smōk/ *n.* a cloud that rises from something that is burning. *The smoke from the fireplace smells good.*

smoke² /smōk/ *v.* (**smokes, smoked, smok•ing**) to give out smoke. *The chimney is smoking.*

smooth /smo͞oth/ *adj.* having no bumps or rough spots. *The smooth highway made driving a pleasure.*

snake /snāk/ *n.* a long, crawling reptile that has scales and no legs. *Some snakes are poisonous.*

snake

snow¹ /snō/ *n.* frozen water crystals that fall to the earth as soft white flakes. *Snow falls in winter.*

snow² /snō/ *v.* to fall as snow. *It has started to snow.*

soak /sōk/ *v.* **a.** to wet through; to make or become wet. *The heavy rain fell for two days, soaking the dry land.* **b.** to let stay in water or other liquid. *The baseball player soaked his sore arm in hot water.*

soap /sōp/ *n.* a substance used for washing. *Use plenty of soap when you wash your hands.*

soft /sôft/ or /sŏft/ *adj.* (**soft•ly,** *adv.*) **a.** not hard. *We can dig easily in this soft ground.* **b.** smooth; not rough. *The baby has soft skin.* **c.** quiet; gentle; mild. *She has a soft voice.*

soil /soil/ *n.* ground; earth; dirt. *Plants grow in rich, dark soil.*

some•one /sŭm′ wŭn′/ or /sŭm′ wən/ *pron.* somebody; some person. *Someone ought to fix that front door.*

some•thing /sŭm′ thĭng/ *pron.* a certain thing that is not specifically named. *Give the dog something to eat.*

song /sông/ or /sŏng/ *n.* a tune; a piece of music to be sung. *The principal asked us to sing another song.*

sor•ry /sŏr′ ē/ or /sôr′ ē/ *adj.* (**sor•ri•er, sor•ri•est; sor•ri•ly,** *adv.*) feeling regret; full of sorrow or sadness. *I'm sorry; I didn't mean to bump you.*

sound¹ /sound/ *n.* anything that is heard; a noise. *The sound of the bells came softly on the breeze.*

sound² /sound/ *v.* to make a noise. *His snores sounded all through the house.*

south /south/ *n.* the direction to the left when a person faces the sunset. *A warm wind blew from the south.*

space /spās/ *n.* **a.** the area in which the planets and stars exist. *Earth travels in space around the sun.* **b.** room; a place. *There is no more space for passengers in the crowded train.*

speech /spēch/ *n.* (**speech•es** *pl.*) a talk given in public. *The President made a speech on television.*

spend /spĕnd/ *v.* (**spends, spent, spend•ing**) **a.** to pay out money. *Never spend more than you earn.* **b.** to pass time. *We spent the weekend at the beach.*

spent /spĕnt/ past tense of **spend.**

splash¹ /splăsh/ *v.* **a.** to scatter and fall in drops. *Rain splashed on the pavement.* **b.** to make wet or dirty. *The car splashed me with mud as it sped past.*

splash² /splăsh/ *n.* (**splash•es** *pl.*) a scattering or throwing of a liquid. *The children made a splash as they jumped into the water.*

spot¹ /spŏt/ *n.* a small mark of a different color. *There's a spot of paint on the rug.*

spot² /spŏt/ *v.* (**spots, spot•ted, spot•ting**) to see; to locate; to catch sight of. *How can we spot him in this big crowd?*

spot•ted /spŏt′ ĭd/ *adj.* having spots. *Heather wore a spotted blouse.*

spring¹ /sprĭng/ *v.* (**springs, sprang, sprung, spring•ing**) **a.** to jump; to leap. *The fox sprang at the rabbit.* **b.** to snap back into position. *A rubber band will spring back instantly.*

spring² /sprĭng/ *n.* **a.** a coil of wire or a strip of metal that goes back into shape after pressure is released. *Does your watch have a spring?* **b.** the season of the year that begins about March 21 and ends about June 21. *The weather begins to get warm in spring.*

stair /stâr/ *n.* a single step of a series of steps going up or down. *When we got to the last stair going up, we were out of breath.*

stamp /stămp/ *n.* a small, printed piece of paper for sticking on letters and packages to show that the postage has been paid. *You can buy a stamp at the post office.*

stamp

stand /stănd/ *v.* (**stands, stood, stand•ing**) **a.** to be or place upright. *Can you stand on one leg?* **b.** to endure; to put up with. *How can you stand such a mess?*

star•fish /stär′ fĭsh′/ *n.* (**star•fish•es** or **star•fish** *pl.*) a small sea animal with a body shaped like a star. *We found a starfish on the beach.*

state /stāt/ *n.* **a.** the condition of. *The old house was in a bad state.* **b.** one of the fifty separate divisions of the United States. *Rhode Island is the smallest state.*

steep /stēp/ *adj.* slanting sharply up and down. *That cliff is too steep to climb.*

stem /stĕm/ *n.* the part of a plant that grows up from the ground; a stalk. *Some roses have long stems.*

stick /stĭk/ *n.* a long, thin piece of wood or other material. *We used a stick to stir the paint.*

sting¹ /stĭng/ *v.* (**stings, stung, sting•ing**) **a.** to prick or wound with a small point. *Bees and wasps sting.* **b.** to affect with a sharp pain. *Soap stings the eyes.*

Pronunciation Key

ă	pat	ŏ	pot	th	**th**in
ā	pay	ō	toe	th	**th**is
âr	care	ô	paw, for	hw	**wh**ich
ä	father	oi	noise	zh	vi**s**ion
ĕ	pet	ou	**ou**t	ə	**a**bout,
ē	be	ŏŏ	took		item,
ĭ	pit	ōō	boot		pencil,
ī	pie	ŭ	cut		gall**o**p,
îr	pier	ûr	**ur**ge		circ**u**s

sting² /stĭng/ *n.* a wound or pain caused by stinging. *The bee sting hurt for three days.*

stitch¹ /stĭch/ *n.* (**stitch•es** *pl.*) one complete movement of a threaded needle through cloth or other material. *Tie a knot after the last stitch.*

stitch² /stĭch/ *v.* (**stitch•es, stitched, stitch•ing**) to sew. *Can you stitch these quilt squares together?*

stone /stōn/ *n.* **a.** rock; hard mineral matter. *Our house is built of stone.* **b.** a small piece of this material; a bit of rock. *We threw stones into the water.* **c.** a gem. *Diamonds are precious stones.*

stop¹ /stŏp/ *v.* (**stops, stopped, stop•ping**) to halt or come to a halt. *The car stopped while we were going uphill.*

stop² /stŏp/ *n.* a halt or a short visit. *We made a stop at the grocery store.*

stop•light /stŏp′ līt/ *n.* a traffic light; a signal. *Turn right at the second stoplight.*

storm /stôrm/ *n.* strong winds often accompanied by heavy amounts of rain, snow, hail, or sleet. *In summer a storm can bring thunder and lightning.*

stor•y /stôr′ ē/ or /stōr′ ē/ *n.* (**stor•ies** *pl.*) a tale or account of an adventure or happening. *Mr. Lee told us a story about his grandfather.*

straw¹ /strô/ *n.* **a.** the hollow stalks or stems of grain, such as wheat or oats, after the grain has been removed. *Straw is used to make baskets.* **b.** a thin hollow tube of plastic or paper. *Karen drank her milk through a straw.*

straw² /strô/ *adj.* made of straw. *She wore a straw hat.*

stream /strēm/ *n.* a brook, creek, or small river. *The stream bubbled over the rocks.*

street /strēt/ *n.* a road in a city or town. *This street is always crowded during rush hour.*

stretch /strĕch/ *v.* **a.** to hold out; to extend. *Rachel stretched her hand across the table.* **b.** to draw out to full length; to extend to full size. *Jeff stretched after he woke up.*

string /strĭng/ *n.* a thin cord; a thick thread. *How much string do you need for your kite?*

strong /strông/ or /strŏng/ *adj.* **a.** not weak; powerful. *We need someone strong to lift this box.* **b.** hard to break or knock down; lasting; tough. *You will need a strong rope.* **c.** not mild; sharp. *Some people like strong cheese.*

stud•y¹ /stŭd′ ē/ *v.* (**stud•ies, stud•ied, stud•y•ing**) to try to learn by thinking, reading, and practicing. *We study many subjects in school.*

stud•y² /stŭd′ ē/ *n.* (**stud•ies** *pl.*) an investigation; an examination. *Our school nurse made a study of our health habits.*

stuff¹ /stŭf/ *n.* things; objects of any kind. *Don't put any more stuff in the car.*

stuff² /stŭf/ *v.* to fill by packing things into. *We stuffed the box with old newspapers.*

sub•tract /səb trăkt′/ *v.* to take away. *If we subtract 7 from 10, we get 3.*

sud•den /sŭd′ n/ *adj.* (**sud•den•ly,** *adv.*) **a.** not expected. *We got caught in the sudden rainfall.* **b.** quick; hasty. *Mr. Parker made a sudden decision.*

sum•mer¹ /sŭm′ ər/ *n.* the warmest season of the year. *Summer comes between spring and fall.*

sum•mer² /sŭm′ ər/ *adj.* of summer; for summer. *Some summer days are very hot.*

sun•ny /sŭn′ ē/ *adj.* (**sun•ni•er, sun•ni•est; sun•ni•ly,** *adv.*) bright with sunshine. *Let's play outside while it's still sunny.*

sun•shine /sŭn′ shīn/ *n.* the light from the sun. *Our cat loves to nap in the sunshine.*

sup•per /sŭp′ ər/ *n.* the last meal of the day. *We hurried home for supper.*

sure /shŏŏr/ *adj.* (**sur•er, sur•est; sure•ly,** *adv.*) certain; positive. *Are you sure the clock shows the correct time?*

swam /swăm/ past tense of **swim.**

sweet /swēt/ *adj.* **a.** having the taste of sugar. *We ate sweet rolls for breakfast.* **b.** pleasing. *I think roses have a sweet smell.*

swim /swĭm/ *v.* (**swims, swam, swum, swim•ming**) to move in water by moving arms, legs, fins, etc. *Fish swim, but so do people.*

swim

switch¹ /swĭch/ *n.* (**switch•es** *pl.*) in an electrical circuit, a device for making a connection. *When we turn the switch, the light goes on.*

switch² /swĭch/ *v.* **a.** to turn on or off. *Please switch the fan off.* **b.** to change. *Let's switch places; you stand here.*

take /tāk/ v. (**takes, took, tak•en, tak•ing**) **a.** to accept or receive. *Take one; they're free.* **b.** to carry. *We took three suitcases.* **c.** to travel on. *Let's take the bus.* **d. take up** to require; to use. *Boxes take up too much space.*

talk¹ /tôk/ v. (**talks, talked, talk•ing**) **a.** to speak; to say words. *My little sister just learned to talk.* **b.** to communicate. *Deaf people sometimes talk with their hands.*

talk² /tôk/ n. **a.** a conversation. *Tim and I had a long talk.* **b.** a short speech. *The scientist gave a talk about fossils.*

teach•er /tē′ chər/ n. a person who teaches. *Who is your piano teacher?*

tear¹ /târ/ v. (**tears, tore, torn, tear•ing**) to rip or pull apart. *We made shapes by tearing pieces of paper.*

tear² /târ/ n. a rip. *There's a tear in the elbow of my jacket.*

tent /tĕnt/ n. a portable structure of canvas or other material supported by a pole or poles. *We sleep in tents when we go hiking.*

test¹ /tĕst/ n. an examination or trial, often consisting of a series of questions or problems. *There were twenty problems on the arithmetic test.*

test² /tĕst/ v. to try; to examine; to put to a test. *Our teacher tested us in history last week.*

that's /thăts/ that is; that has.

their /thâr/ adj. of, belonging to, or relating to them. *Is that your cat or their cat?*

▶ **Their** sounds like **there**.

there¹ /thâr/ adv. **a.** in or at that place. *Put the flowers over there.* **b.** to that place; into that place. *I went there last week.*

Pronunciation Key

ă	p**a**t	ŏ	p**o**t	th	**th**in
ā	p**ay**	ō	t**oe**	th	**th**is
âr	c**are**	ô	p**aw**, f**or**	hw	**wh**ich
ä	f**a**ther	oi	n**oi**se	zh	vi**s**ion
ĕ	p**e**t	ou	**ou**t	ə	**a**bout,
ē	b**e**	o͝o	t**oo**k		it**e**m,
ĭ	p**i**t	o͞o	b**oo**t		penc**i**l,
ī	p**ie**	ŭ	c**u**t		gall**o**p,
îr	p**ier**	ûr	**ur**ge		circ**u**s

there² /thâr/ pron. used to introduce a sentence or clause in which the subject follows the verb. *There is a new student in our class.*

▶ **There** sounds like **their**.

there's /thârz/ there is; there has.

thick /thĭk/ adj. **a.** large in size from one side to its opposite; not thin. *The old castle door was very thick.* **b.** measuring in distance through; in depth. *The geography book is one inch thick.*

thing /thĭng/ n. **a.** any object; anything that exists and can be seen, heard, felt, etc. *He took his clothes and some other things to summer camp.* **b.** an action; a matter; an affair. *That was a good thing to do.*

think /thĭngk/ v. (**thinks, thought, think•ing**) **a.** to use the mind to reach decisions, form opinions, etc. *I can't think when there is noise all around me.* **b.** to have in mind as an opinion, idea, etc.; to believe. *She thought she knew the answer.*

thir•ty-two /thûr′ tē too͞′/ n. the next number after thirty-one; thirty plus two; 32. *There are only thirty-two cards in the deck.*

thorn /thôrn/ n. a sharp point that grows on the stems and branches of some plants. *He cut his finger on a thorn while he was trimming the rose bushes.*

thorn

threw /thrōo/ past tense of **throw**.

throw¹ /thrō/ v. (**throws, threw, thrown, throw•ing**) to toss or cast through the air. *Throw the ball to Angie.*

throw² /thrō/ n. an act of throwing; a toss. *The player made a bad throw to first base and the runner was safe.*

thumb /thŭm/ n. **a.** the short, thick finger on the hand. *Little Jack Horner stuck his thumb into his pie.* **b.** something that covers the thumb. *Someone cut the thumbs off my mittens.*

thumb

to•day¹ /tə dā'/ n. this present day; the present time. *Today is the first day of spring.*

to•day² /tə dā'/ adv. on this present day. *Are you going to school today?*

to•mor•row¹ /tə mŏr' ō/ or /tə môr' ō/ n. the day after today. *Tomorrow is the last day of school.*

to•mor•row² /tə mŏr' ō/ or /tə môr' ō/ adv. on the day after today. *We're going shopping tomorrow.*

tongue /tŭng/ n. a wide, flat organ in the mouth made of flesh and muscle and capable of easy movement. *The doctor looked at my tongue.*

to•night¹ /tə nīt'/ n. the night of the present day. *Tonight is a special night.*

to•night² /tə nīt'/ adv. on the night of the present day. *Let's go to a movie tonight.*

tooth•paste /tooth' pāst'/ n. paste used to clean the teeth. *My dentist told me to use a toothpaste with fluoride in it.*

tore /tôr/ or /tōr/ past tense of **tear**.

tote /tōt/ v. (**totes, tot•ed, tot•ing**) *Informal.* to haul; to carry. *The farmer said he had to tote some hay up to the barn.*

town /toun/ n. **a.** a center of population that is larger than a village but smaller than a city. *Our cousins live in a small town in Kansas.* **b.** a city. *He decided that Chicago was his favorite town.*

trace /trās/ v. (**trac•es, traced, trac•ing**) to copy by placing transparent paper over a picture and following the lines of the picture with a pencil or pen. *We were told to draw a map, not to trace one.*

track /trăk/ n. **a.** a mark or a series of marks left by an animal, person, wagon, etc. *We saw the tire tracks on the snow.* **b.** a special path or course set up for racing. *A mile is four times around the track.* **c.** the metal rails on which trains run. *The railroad track runs through a tunnel.*

trade¹ /trād/ n. **a.** the business of buying and selling goods. *Our company carries on trade with people all over the world.* **b.** an exchange of goods; a bargain. *I made a trade with him.*

trade² /trād/ v. (**trades, trad•ed, trad•ing**) **a.** to buy and sell goods. *Some companies trade with foreign countries.* **b.** to exchange. *I'll trade my pen for that book.*

trail¹ /trāl/ n. a path through mountains, a forest, etc. *The trail ended at the edge of the cliff.*

trail² /trāl/ v. to follow or pursue by following tracks or traces left behind. *The police trailed the suspect.*

tray /trā/ n. a flat holder or platform with a rim, used for holding or carrying something. *Put the dishes on a tray.*

treat¹ /trēt/ v. **a.** to handle; behave toward. *You must treat animals gently.* **b.** to try to cure or relieve. *The doctor treated me for the pain in my stomach.*

treat² /trēt/ n. anything that pleases or gives pleasure. *Seeing a movie at school was a special treat.*

tries /trīz/ a form of **try**.

trip¹ /trĭp/ *n.* a journey; a voyage. *They took a trip around the world last year.*

trip² /trĭp/ *v.* (**trips, tripped, trip•ping**) to lose one's balance by catching a foot on something. *I tripped on the edge of the rug.*

try¹ /trī/ *v.* (**tries, tried, try•ing**) to attempt. *Try to answer all of the questions.*

try² /trī/ *n.* (**tries** *pl.*) an attempt; an effort to do something. *She hit the target on her first try.*

turn¹ /tûrn/ *v.* **a.** to move or cause to move around a center; to rotate. *Wheels turn.* **b.** to change directions. *Turn left at the post office.*

turn² /tûrn/ *n.* **a.** a change in direction or condition. *Make a right turn at the next street.* **b.** a time to do something. *Whose turn is it to bat?*

tur•tle /tûr′ tl/ *n.* an animal having four legs and a hard shell around its body. *A turtle can draw its head and legs into its shell.*

twen•ty-four /twĕn′ tē fôr′/ or /twĕn′ tē fōr′/ *n.* the next number after twenty-three; twenty plus four; 24. *In some places clocks go from one to twenty-four.*

twig /twĭg/ *n.* a very small branch of a tree or other plant. *We used twigs to get the campfire started.*

un•cle /ŭng′ kəl/ *n.* **a.** the brother of one's father or mother. *I have two uncles on my mother's side.* **b.** the husband of one's aunt. *We visited our aunt and uncle last spring.*

un•der /ŭn′ dər/ *prep.* **a.** below; beneath. *I found money hidden under a rock.* **b.** less than. *You can repair the broken window for under forty dollars.*

un•der•stand /ŭn′ dər stănd′/ *v.* (**un•der•stands, un•der•stood, un•der•stand•ing**) to get the meaning; to grasp the idea. *Do you understand all the test directions?*

United States *n.* a country in North America that lies between the Atlantic and Pacific oceans and between Canada and the Gulf of Mexico; it includes Hawaii and Alaska. *The flag of the United States is red, white, and blue.*

United States flag

un•til¹ /ŭn tĭl′/ *prep.* **a.** up to the time of; till. *I slept until noon today.* **b.** before the time of. *He could not stop working until midnight.*

un•til² /ŭn tĭl′/ *conj.* **a.** up to the time that. *We waited for you until the show was about to begin.* **b.** before. *She would not serve dinner until everyone was seated.*

up•on /ə pŏn′/ or /ə pôn′/ *prep.* on. *Place the book upon the table.*

vac•cine /văk sēn′/ *n.* a mixture intro-duced into the body to protect against disease. *Most children receive the vac-cine against polio when they are very young.*

veg•e•ta•ble /věj′ tə bəl/ or /věj′ ĭ tə bəl/ *n.* a plant or a part of a plant that is used as food. *Peas and beans are vegetables.*

ver•y /věr′ ē/ *adv.* greatly; extremely. *He was very unhappy when he lost his dog.*

voice /vois/ *n.* **a.** a sound made with the mouth, especially by talking or singing. *We heard her voice above all the others.* **b.** the type or quality of sound made with the mouth. *That singer has a pleasant voice.*

walk¹ /wôk/ *v.* to go on foot at a nor-mal rate. *Scott ran ahead, but the rest of us walked.*

walk² /wôk/ *n.* **a.** the act of walking. *Would you like to go for a walk with me?* **b.** the distance one has to walk. *It is just a short walk to the grocery store.*

war /wôr/ *n.* a fight or struggle between countries or parts of a country. *There are great losses of life and destruction of property in a war.*

▶ **War** sounds like **wore.**

warm¹ /wôrm/ *adj.* **a.** having a small amount of heat; neither hot nor cold. *Blankets keep us warm.* **b.** affectionate. *They gave us a warm greeting.*

warm² /wôrm/ *v.* to make warm; to heat. *Warm the food before you serve it.*

wasp /wŏsp/ or /wôsp/ *n.* a flying insect with a slender body and a painful sting. *Wasps build papery nests.*

watch¹ /wŏch/ *v.* **a.** to look at. *Did you watch television after school?* **b.** to pay attention to; to be careful. *Watch where you are going.*

watch² /wŏch/ *n.* (**watch•es** *pl.*) a small clock that is worn on the wrist or carried in a pocket. *I checked my watch before I left the house.*

wave¹ /wāv/ *n.* **a.** a rising swell of water moving across the sur-face of a body of water. *The waves splashed against the rocks.* **b.** a signal made with the hand. *He gave a wave as he passed us.*

wave

wave² /wāv/ *v.* (**waves, waved, wav•ing**) **a.** to move up and down or from side to side. *The branches waved in the wind.* **b.** to give a signal or greet-ing by moving the hand. *We waved good-bye.*

way /wā/ *n.* **a.** a path, road, or course. *The way was blocked by a fallen tree.* **b.** direction. *Come this way.* **c.** distance. *It's only a short way from here.* **d.** a man-ner. *She has a funny way of talking.* **e.** a detail or feature. *In many ways his plan seemed good.*

▶ **Way** sounds like **weigh.**

wear /wâr/ *v.* (**wears, wore, worn, wear•ing**) **a.** to have on the body. *People wear clothes.* **b.** to make or pro-duce gradually as a result of rubbing, scraping, etc. *He wore a hole in the sleeve of his sweater.*

weath•er /wěth′ ər/ *n.* outside condi-tions of temperature, humidity, etc. *We have had two weeks of cold weather.*

weigh /wā/ *v.* **a.** to determine the weight of by using a scale. *Weigh the package before you mail it.* **b.** to have weight of a certain amount. *She weighs eighty pounds.*

▶ **Weigh** sounds like **way.**

were /wûr/ past tense of **be.**

west¹ /wĕst/ *n.* the direction in which the sun sets. *East and west are opposite directions.*

west² /wĕst/ *adj.* **a.** in the west; of the west; toward the west. *Cindy lives in the west part of town.* **b.** from the west. *A west wind was blowing.*

west³ /wĕst/ *adv.* toward the west. *We walked west.*

whale /hwāl/ *n.* a huge sea mammal that looks like a fish and breathes air. *When a whale comes up for air, it blows a spout of water vapor.*

whale

what's /hwŏts/ or /hwŭts/ what is; what has.

wheel /hwēl/ or /wēl/ *n.* a round frame that turns on a central axis. *A bicycle has two wheels.*

where¹ /hwâr/ or /wâr/ *adv.* **a.** in or at what place. *Where will you be?* **b.** to what place. *Where did you go?*

where² /hwâr/ or /wâr/ *conj.* to the place that; in the place that. *Stay where you are.*

who's /ho͞oz/ who is; who has.

wide /wīd/ *adj.* (**wid•er, wid•est; wide•ly,** *adv.*) **a.** covering or having much space from side to side; broad; not narrow. *Our new car has wide seats.* **b.** having a certain distance from side to side. *My room is ten feet wide.*

wild /wīld/ *adj.* not tamed; not cultivated; living or growing in a natural condition. *Wild flowers grew along the side of the road.*

Pronunciation Key

ă	pat	ŏ	pot	th	**th**in
ā	pay	ō	toe	th	**th**is
âr	care	ô	paw, for	hw	**wh**ich
ä	father	oi	noise	zh	vision
ĕ	pet	ou	out	ə	about,
ē	be	o͝o	took		item,
ĭ	pit	o͞o	boot		pencil,
ī	pie	ŭ	cut		gallop,
îr	pier	ûr	urge		circus

will /wĭl/ *v.* (**would**) **a.** am, is, or are going to. *We will see you next week.* **b.** am, is, or are willing to. *I'll help if you will.*

win•dow /wĭn' dō/ *n.* an opening in the side of a house, automobile, etc., usually covered with glass. *Windows let in light and air.*

with•out /wĭth out'/ *prep.* **a.** not having; with no. *I left without my umbrella.* **b.** with a lack or neglect of. *I sometimes speak without thinking.*

wom•an /wo͝om' ən/ *n.* (**wom•en** *pl.*) a grown female person. *Your mother is a woman.*

wom•en /wĭm' ĭn/ plural of **woman.**

won't /wōnt/ will not.

word /wûrd/ *n.* a group of letters that make sense because they stand for a certain thing. *We use words when we speak and write.*

wore /wôr/ or /wōr/ past tense of **wear.**

▶ **Wore** sounds like **war.**

work¹ /wûrk/ *n.* **a.** the use of strength or skill to make or do something; labor. *Building the dam was hard work for the beavers.* **b.** job; occupation; the thing one does to earn a living. *Her work is modeling clothes.*

work² /wûrk/ *v.* **a.** to have a job for pay in order to make a living. *He works in a big office.* **b.** to operate; to do as it should. *Does that machine work?*

work•er /wûr′ kər/ *n.* a person who works; a person who works for money. *The factory needs more workers.*

wor•ry[1] /wûr′ ē/ or /wŭr′ ē/ *v.* (**wor•ries, wor•ried, wor•ry•ing**) to be or cause to be restless, disturbed, or anxious about something. *I am worried about getting to the airport on time.*

wor•ry[2] /wûr′ ē/ or /wŭr′ ē/ *n.* (**wor•ries** *pl.*) a cause of anxiety or trouble. *Money is a constant worry to him.*

would /wŏŏd/ *v.* **a.** used to express what could have happened or been true. *I would have come if I had known you were sick.* **b.** used to make a polite request. *Would you carry this for me?* **c.** past tense of **will**.

wrap /răp/ *v.* (**wraps, wrapped, wrap•ping**) **a.** to enclose in something by winding or folding. *Wrap the baby in warm blankets.* **b.** to cover with paper. *Did you wrap the gift for your mother?*

wrist /rĭst/ *n.* the joint between the hand and the arm. *The wrist can move in any direction.*

write /rīt/ *v.* (**writes, wrote, writ•ten, writ•ing**) **a.** to form letters or words with a pen, pencil, or other instrument. *Most people learn to write in school.* **b.** to be the author of. *He wrote a story for the school newspaper.*
▶ **Write** sounds like **right**.

wrote /rōt/ past tense of **write**.

yes•ter•day[1] /yĕs′ tər dā/ or /yĕs′ tər dē/ *n.* the day before this day. *Today is Saturday and yesterday was Friday.*

yes•ter•day[2] /yĕs′ tər dā/ or /yĕs′ tər dē/ *adv.* on the day before this. *It snowed yesterday.*

your /yŏŏr/ or /yôr/ *adj.* of or belonging to you. *Is this your coat?*

ze•bra /zē′ brə/ *n.* a wild member of the horse family that has stripes of black or dark brown on a light background. *Zebras are difficult to tame.*

zebra

USING THE Thesaurus

The **Writing Thesaurus** gives synonyms, or words that mean the same or nearly the same, and antonyms, or words that mean the opposite, for your spelling words. Use this sample to learn about the different parts of each thesaurus entry.

- **Entry words** are given in alphabetical order and are shown in boldface type.

- The abbreviation for the **part of speech** of each entry word follows the boldface entry word.

- The **definition** of the entry word explains the word's meaning. A **sample sentence** shows you how to use the word.

- Each **synonym** of the entry word is listed under the entry word. Again, a sample sentence shows the correct use of the synonym.

- Sometimes, an **antonym** for the entry word is listed at the end of the entry.

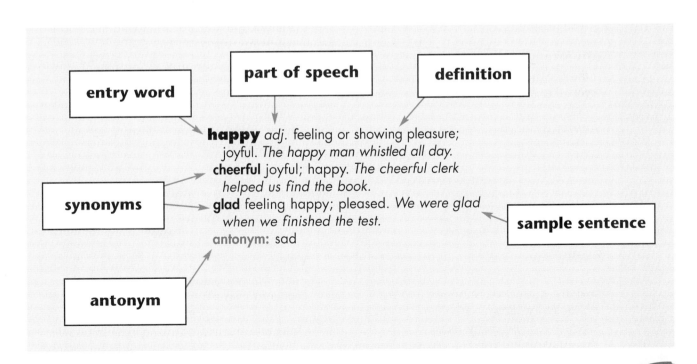

entry word

part of speech

definition

happy *adj.* feeling or showing pleasure; joyful. *The happy man whistled all day.*
cheerful joyful; happy. *The cheerful clerk helped us find the book.*
glad feeling happy; pleased. *We were glad when we finished the test.*
antonym: sad

synonyms

sample sentence

antonym

about *adv.* somewhere near. *She guessed it was about seven o'clock.*
  almost nearly; just about. *That bus is almost on time; it is only two minutes late.*
  nearly almost; not quite. *We were nearly finished with our homework.*
  roughly somewhat like. *The houses looked roughly alike.*

afraid *adj.* frightened; filled with fear. *Some people are afraid of falling from high places.*
  alarmed filled with sudden fear. *The man was alarmed by the loud noise.*
  fearful showing fear. *The fearful kitten raced to its mother.*
  frightened full of fright. *The frightened child hid from the very scary creature.*

after *prep.* following. *Don't forget that you come after me in the parade.*
  behind farther back. *We will march behind the clowns.*
  following coming after. *The parade will take place the following day.*
  next following at once. *You will have the next turn.*

always *adv.* all the time; constantly. *At the North Pole, it is always cold.*
  ever at any time. *Have you ever traveled to Europe?*
  forever for always. *People want to be healthy forever.*

badly *adv.* poorly; in a bad manner. *He plays the piano well but sings badly.*
  awfully in an awful manner; terribly. *Usually the clowns are funny, but they acted awfully rowdy today.*
  dreadfully in a dreadful manner. *The actor played his part dreadfully.*

poorly in a poor manner. *The football team played poorly today.*

band *n.* any flat strip of material used for holding something together. *Put a rubber band around each newspaper.*
  sash long, broad strip of cloth worn around the waist. *The dress has a red flowered sash.*
  strap a thin strip of leather or another type of material. *I put a strap around the suitcase.*

better *adj.* higher in quality; more excellent; finer. *Does anyone have a better place?*
  improved made better. *The mayor told about the improved condition of the city budget.*
  superior very good; above average. *She did superior work as an officer.*

blow *v.* to move rapidly. *We could hear the wind blow.*
  blast to blow up; tear apart. *They had to blast the rocks for the new roadway.*
  toot to give a short blast. *The horn will toot at lunchtime.*

bright *adj.* shining; giving light; reflecting light. *See how bright the car is when it is polished.*
  brilliant sparkling; shining brightly. *A brilliant light shone in the sky.*
  clear bright; light. *You could see the plane fly across the clear sky.*
  light clear; bright. *It is as light as day in here.*
  shiny bright; shining. *The shiny vase sparkled in the sunlight.*

care *n.* protection; close attention. *A baby needs loving care.*
  concern interest; attention. *Our main concern was using the right words.*
  interest a feeling of taking part in or wanting to know. *The students had an interest in space travel.*

worry a cause of anxiety or trouble. *Money is a constant worry to him.*

carry *v.* to take from one place to another. *Will you carry this package home?*
conduct to carry or transfer. *The wires conduct electricity from the wall to the lamp.*
transport to carry from one place to another. *A truck was used to transport the new cars.*

catch *v.* to get; take and hold onto; seize. *Watch the boy catch the ball!*
capture to take by force. *The zookeeper will capture the runaway animal.*
seize to grasp; take hold of. *The happy child tried to seize the big balloon.*

change *v.* to make or become different. *She will change her mind.*
alter to make different. *We can alter our plans for the trip to the zoo.*
vary to change; become different. *I will vary the colors in the picture.*

choose *v.* to pick out. *Choose the kind of toy you want.*
elect to choose for an office by voting. *Who did the group elect as class president?*
pick to make a choice. *I will pick the winner of the contest.*
select to choose; pick out. *The teacher will select a book about the stars.*

close *v.* to shut. *Close the door when you leave.*
bolt to fasten with a bolt. *She will bolt the door each night.*
seal to close tightly; shut. *He tried to seal the box with tape.*
shut to close; to prevent entrance. *We shut the door to the gym.*

cost *n.* price that is to be paid. *The cost of meals in restaurants is going up.*
amount the value; sum. *The amount on the bill was twenty dollars.*
charge price for service; cost. *A delivery charge will be added to the furniture bill.*
price the cost in money; the amount of money for which something is sold. *The price should be clearly labeled.*

dawn *n.* the first appearance of light in the morning. *Dawn came at six o'clock this morning.*
daybreak time when light appears in the morning. *The rooster crowed at daybreak.*
sunrise time when the sun appears in the sky. *The campers got up at sunrise.*

digging *v.* making a hole in the ground; breaking up the soil. *The dog was digging in the backyard.*
burrowing making a hole in the ground. *We caught a rabbit burrowing under the fence.*
tunneling making a way under the ground. *Moles are tunneling under the whole backyard!*

draw *v.* to make a design, picture, etc. *The artist will draw an outline before he paints the picture.*
design to make a sketch or a plan. *She will design a new skirt.*
outline to give a sketch; plan. *We must outline our ideas for the report.*
sketch to make a rough drawing. *The builder will sketch the plans.*

dream *n.* the thoughts, feelings, and pictures that occur in a person's mind as he or she sleeps. *Her dream was about flying in an airplane.*
nightmare a very troubled dream. *The terrible nightmare made him scream.*
vision something seen in one's imagination, dreams, or thoughts. *He had a vision that he was the new captain.*

drop *v.* to fall or let fall. *I will try not to drop a dish as I dry it.*
fall to drop from a higher place. *The leaves fall from the trees.*
lower to put down. *Use the rope to lower the flag.*

dull *adj.* uninteresting; boring. *It was such a dull book that I fell asleep reading it.*
boring dull; tiresome. *The boring play had no exciting action in it.*
tiresome tiring; boring. *Without any good jokes, the clown's act was very tiresome.*
uninteresting not interesting. *With no points scored, it was a very uninteresting game.*

early *adv.* sooner than usual; before the usual time. *I will have to get up early to go fishing tomorrow.*
shortly before long. *The parade will start shortly.*
soon in a short time; before the usual time; early. *The bus arrived much too soon.*
antonym: late

earn *v.* to deserve as a result of performing a service, doing work, etc. *After we study for two hours, we will earn a break.*
merit to earn; deserve. *The careful workers merit the award for their excellent safety record.*
rate to consider, regard; put a value on. *We rate the movie the best science show of the year.*

fair *adj.* in keeping with the rules; according to what is accepted as right. *If you want to play on the team, you must learn fair play.*
equal of the same value, size, rank, amount, etc. *The two boys are of equal weight.*
just right; fair. *She received a just reward for her heroic deeds.*
reasonable not asking too much; just. *We paid a reasonable price for the bookcases.*
antonym: unfair

fight *v.* to try to overcome by force. *Boxers wear padded gloves when they fight.*
battle to take part in a fight or struggle. *The team will battle for first place.*
clash to disagree strongly; fight. *The report's viewpoint always seems to clash with ours.*

find *v.* to look for and get back a lost object. *We will find my watch.*
discover to find out; learn for the first time. *The hikers want to discover a new trail in the woods.*
locate to find the specific place. *The museum guide helped us locate the dinosaur display.*
antonym: lose

finish *v.* to come or bring to an end; complete or become completed. *The movie will finish at 9:30.*
complete to finish; get done. *We will complete the job before we go home.*
conclude to come or bring to an end. *The speaker will conclude by asking everyone to help with the book fair.*
end to stop; to come or bring to its last part. *Our story will end with a very clever surprise.*
antonyms: start, begin

flash *n.* a light that appears suddenly and briefly. *A flash of lightning appeared in the distance.*
gleam a flash or beam of light. *You could see the gleam of the car's lights through the fog.*
sparkle shine; glitter; flash. *The sparkle of the jewels caught my eye.*

float *v.* to stay or move in or on top of air, water, or liquid. *Ice will float in water.*
drift to carry or be carried along by air or water. *The wind made the balloons drift toward the trees.*
antonym: sink

flow *v.* to move in a stream, as water does. *A river can flow to the ocean.*
run to flow. *Water will run downhill.*
stream to flow, move. *The tears seemed to stream down his face.*

fool *v.* to trick or attempt to trick someone. *Her costume could not fool me into thinking she was someone else.*
deceive to mislead; trick. *The magician tried to deceive us with his magic tricks.*
trick to fool; cheat. *We will trick them into thinking the painting was real.*

fresh *adj.* newly made, grown, or gathered. *Mother baked fresh bread.*
new not having existed before. *We played with the new computer game.*
unusual not ordinary. *The book was an unusual size.*
antonym: stale

friend *n.* a person one likes. *Julio is a good friend.*
companion someone close to another; someone to share with. *Jane's dog is her favorite companion.*
comrade a close friend. *The officer and her comrade directed traffic.*
mate a fellow worker or companion. *My trusted mate helped with the work.*
pal a friend; comrade. *My pal and I like to play baseball.*

funny *adj.* strange; unusual; peculiar. *That is a funny way to act.*
curious odd; unusual. *We heard the curious noises from the haunted house.*
odd strange; peculiar. *The music was odd because it had no melody.*
peculiar unusual; strange. *Having a snake for a pet is somewhat peculiar.*

furry *adj.* covered with fur. *A mouse is a very small, furry animal.*
bushy thick; spreading. *The pirate's beard was very bushy.*
hairy covered with hair. *The dog has a hairy body.*
woolly covered with wool or something like it. *The sheep had a woolly coat.*

give *v.* to hand over to another as a present. *Please give me the watch.*
award to give; present. *He will award a prize to the best writer.*
donate to give help or money; contribute. *We will donate our time to clean the park.*
present to offer; give. *The track coach will present ribbons to the winning teams.*
antonym: take

grand *adj.* large; beautiful; impressive. *The queen lived in a grand palace.*
magnificent stately; grand. *The royal family lived in a magnificent castle by the river.*
majestic noble; grand. *The queen rode in a majestic carriage.*
splendid brilliant; grand. *The picture showed a splendid view of the palace.*

great *adj.* large in size or number; big. *A great crowd of people was at the carnival.*
enormous huge; very large. *The enormous crowd clapped for the clowns.*
immense very large; huge. *The immense elephant stood by the tiny mouse.*
large big. *A whale is large.*
vast very great; large. *The animals roamed through the vast jungle.*

hair *n.* the mass of thin threadlike strands that grow on a person's or animal's skin. *Elizabeth has beautiful hair.*
curl a lock of hair forming a ring. *She tucked a curl behind her ear.*
locks the hair on one's head. *She tied a ribbon around her curly locks.*

happy *adj.* feeling or showing pleasure; joyful. *The happy man whistled all day.*
cheerful joyful; happy. *The cheerful clerk helped us find the book.*
glad feeling happy; pleased. *We were glad when we finished the test.*
antonym: sad

high *adj.* tall; far above the ground. *Walnuts fell from a high branch.*
tall having great height. *The tall building could be seen for miles.*
towering very high. *They climbed up the towering mountain.*
antonym: low

hop *v.* to move by jumping. *Rabbits hop from place to place.*
bound to leap or spring. *The sheep bound from rock to rock.*
leap to jump. *The tiger can leap over the fallen tree.*
spring to jump; to leap. *The fox will spring at the rabbit.*

hurry *v.* to act quickly; move fast. *Hurry or you'll be late.*
fly to move quickly, swiftly. *We were so busy that the time seemed to fly.*
hustle to move fast; hurry. *We had to hustle to get to the bus stop on time.*

hurt *v.* to cause pain to. *The sting of the bee hurt his arm.*
ache to be in pain; hurt. *His arm must ache after he fell off his bike.*
pain to suffer; hurt. *The sore finger seemed to pain her when she wrote.*
smart to feel sharp pain. *His eyes will smart from the dust in the air.*

ice *n.* water that has been frozen solid by cold. *Ice keeps food and drinks cold.*
glaze a smooth, glossy coating. *The glaze is what makes the dishes shine.*
hail small pieces of ice falling like rain. *The hail beat on the windows.*
sleet snow or hail mixed with rain. *The sleet covered the town with a shiny coat of ice.*

jelly *n.* a food made by boiling fruit juices and sugar. *I like grape jelly.*
jam food made by boiling fruit and sugar until thick. *The jam was full of purple grapes.*
preserves fruit cooked with sugar and sealed in containers. *We put strawberry preserves on our toast.*

join *v.* to put together; to connect. *They will join the caboose to the last car of the train.*
combine to put two or more things together. *The chef will combine the meat and vegetables for the stew.*
link to connect or join. *The chain will link the gate and the fence.*

kind *adj.* gentle and caring. *They are always very kind to animals.*
gentle kindly; friendly. *The teacher spoke with a gentle voice.*
good-hearted caring; generous. *The good-hearted neighbor helped.*

Writing Thesaurus

last *adj.* coming after all others; final. *The last train leaves at six o'clock.*
  concluding bringing to an end. *The concluding question asked for the name of the president.*
  final at the end; coming last. *The final act of the play was exciting.*

lastly *adv.* at the end; finally. *Lastly, pour the batter into a cake pan and put it into the oven.*
  finally at last; at the end. *We finally found the missing ring.*

learn *v.* to gain skill or knowledge in. *We learn spelling in school.*
  acquire to obtain. *She wants to acquire the skills to read another language.*
  master to become skillful; to learn. *He can master the addition facts.*
  study to try to learn by thinking, reading, and practicing. *We study many subjects in school.*

leave *v.* to go away; to go from. *The train will leave in ten minutes.*
  abandon to leave and not return. *The people were told to abandon the ship.*
  desert to leave without notice. *The officer will not desert her post.*
  antonym: arrive

lesson *n.* something to be taught or learned. *My brother is taking his violin lesson.*
  exercise something that gives practice. *The assignment was a math exercise.*
  lecture a planned speech on a topic. *The lecture was on safety.*

letter *n.* a symbol for a sound. *Z is the twenty-sixth letter in our alphabet.*
  character letter, mark, or sign used in writing. *What is the Chinese character for "happy"?*
  symbol something that stands for something else. *The + sign is a symbol used in math.*

lift *v.* to raise from a lower to a higher position. *This box is too heavy for me to lift.*
  elevate to raise up; lift. *The worker used the crane to elevate the heavy beam to the top of the building.*
  hoist to raise; lift up. *The sailors will hoist the sails to begin the trip.*
  raise to put up; lift up. *We had to raise our hands if we wanted a turn.*

list *v.* to write or print in a column. *List the spelling words on your paper.*
  enter to write or print in a book. *You need to enter the addresses by the names.*
  record to write or put in some form. *The scorekeeper will record each score.*

little *adj.* small. *An elephant is big and an ant is little.*
  brief lasting a short time; little. *A brief meeting was held.*
  small not large; little. *The hummingbird is a very small bird.*
  tiny very little; wee. *The tiny ladybug sat on the leaf.*
  antonyms: big, large

load *n.* something that is carried. *The load was too heavy for the small car.*
  cargo goods sent by plane or ship. *The cargo was unloaded from the plane.*
  freight goods carried by plane, truck, ship, or train. *The dock worker sent the freight by truck.*
  shipment goods sent together to a company or person. *The shipment arrived this morning.*

mail *v.* to send by mail; to place in a mailbox. *Did you mail my letter?*
  send to cause or order to go. *The principal might send the children home early because of the storm.*
  transmit to send; to pass along. *The clerk will transmit the order by computer.*

maybe *adv.* perhaps. *Maybe he hasn't left the train yet, and we can still find him.*

perhaps could be; maybe. *Perhaps you will get the first ticket.*

possibly perhaps; by a possibility. *Possibly that is the winning number.*

mild *adj.* not harsh; not severe; warm rather than cold. *We had a mild winter last year.*

calm still; quiet. *Without any wind, the water was calm.*

easy smooth and pleasant. *Her quiet, easy way made everyone around her feel comfortable.*

gentle not rough or violent; mild. *A gentle breeze blew through the trees.*

morning *n.* the earliest part of the day, ending at noon. *We eat breakfast every morning.*

forenoon part of day from sunrise to noon. *We spent the forenoon in the park.*

antonym: evening

news *n.* information; things that a person has not heard about. *What is the news about your brother's new job?*

information knowledge about some fact or event. *The information contains a description of the space launch.*

report information about something seen, heard, done, or read. *The report had many interesting details.*

night *n.* the time between evening and morning; the time from sunset to sunrise when it is dark. *The stars shine at night.*

evening early part of night. *Each evening we eat dinner.*

nighttime time between sunset and morning. *Nighttime begins at dark.*

antonym: day

oil *n.* a greasy liquid obtained from animals, plants, or minerals. *Olive oil is used for salads.*

lubricant oil or grease put on parts of machines to help them move or slide easily. *The mechanic put a lubricant in the engine.*

petroleum a dark liquid found in the earth's crust. *Gasoline is made from petroleum.*

page *n.* one side of a sheet of paper in a book, magazine, newspaper, or letter. *Kurt knew from the first page that he would like the book.*

leaf one sheet of paper. *Each side of a leaf is called a page.*

sheet one piece of paper. *He used one sheet of paper.*

pail *n.* a round bucket with a handle. *He put water in the pail.*

bucket a pail made of plastic, metal, or wood. *The water was in a big bucket.*

scuttle a bucket for carrying or storing coal. *A scuttle was used to store the coal by the old cookstove.*

paint *v.* to cover a surface with paint. *They will paint the fence.*

color to give color; put color on. *He wants to color the fire engine red.*

draw to make a design, picture, etc. *The artist will draw an outline before he paints the picture.*

pair *n.* two things of the same kind that go together; a set of two. *Carlos has a new pair of shoes.*

couple two of anything; a pair. *We saw a couple stumble during the lively dance.*

double person or thing like another. *A person who looks like and can act for an actor is called a double.*

mate a pair. *He could not find the mate to his glove.*

peace *n.* quiet and calm; stillness. *We like the peace of the country.*

calm stillness; quiet. *There was a strange calm before the storm hit.*

quiet stillness; peace. *I need quiet to be able to study.*

serenity calmness; peace and quiet. *We enjoyed the serenity of the countryside.*

antonym: war

people *n.* human beings; persons; men, women, boys, and girls. *People of all ages attended the fair.*

folks people or group of people. *The city folks come to work by bus.*

population number of people in a specific place. *The population of our town is 3,500 people.*

public all the people. *The public was invited to the free concert.*

place *n.* a certain point; a spot. *The coolest place is near the river.*

location place or position. *This is a good location for a repair shop.*

point place or spot. *The race starts at this point.*

spot place. *This is the spot where we can set up the tent.*

place *v.* to put in a particular position; to set. *Place your pencil on the desk.*

put to set at a particular place. *I put the books back on the bookshelf.*

rest to set or place. *He can rest the ladder against the tree.*

set to put in some place or position. *I set the dishes in the sink.*

plain *adj.* simple; not fancy in appearance. *Tracey wore a plain dress.*

modest humble; not bold. *The modest child did not brag about her talent.*

point *v.* to aim. *He meant to point his arrow at the target.*

aim to point or direct. *We tried to aim the telescope at the moon.*

beam to send out; direct. *The machine will beam the light at the sign.*

direct to point or aim. *Direct the light at the sign.*

level to keep even; to aim. *The soldier will level his weapon at the target.*

train to point or aim. *He tried to train the light on the actor.*

pool *n.* a tank filled with water and used for swimming. *Peter swam across the pool.*

basin very shallow water area. *The boats docked in the basin of the harbor.*

lagoon pond or small lake. *The boat was anchored in the lagoon.*

pond a very small lake. *The ducks swam across the pond.*

pretty *adj.* lovely; pleasing; pleasant to look at or to hear. *The garden was filled with pretty flowers.*

attractive pleasing; lovely. *The attractive person modeled new fall clothes.*

beautiful very pretty; pleasing. *The beautiful queen wore a blue dress.*

lovely very pretty; beautiful. *The lovely flowers filled the room with color.*

prize *n.* a thing won in a contest. *Tony won the prize for spelling the most words correctly.*

award prize; something given after careful selection. *The award went to the student with the best test score.*

medal prize; award. *The best swimmer won a gold medal.*

reward payment offered for the return of property or a person. *We got a reward for finding the ring.*

proud *adj.* having satisfaction and pleasure. *The proud mother watched her daughter graduate.*

  exalted filled with pride and joy. *Everyone was exalted by the victory of their beloved king.*

  lofty very high; proud. *The group had set lofty goals for the safety project.*

real *adj.* actual; true; not imagined; not made up. *My uncle told us a real story about his trip to Brazil.*

  actual real; made of facts. *The book tells of actual events in history.*

  factual true; consisting of facts. *She wrote a factual report.*

  true real; genuine. *This is a true story of the life of the queen.*

ribbon *n.* a narrow strip of fabric, especially one used as a decoration. *She wore a yellow ribbon in her hair.*

  braid a narrow band of fabric used to trim clothing. *The uniform is trimmed with a gold braid.*

  tape a narrow strip of material. *The seams had tape on the edges.*

right *adj.* correct; true; accurate. *Allan's answers were all right.*

  accurate exact; correct. *The man gave a very accurate description of the football game.*

  correct right; without errors. *I gave you the correct answer.*

  proper fitting; right for the occasion. *This is not proper behavior at a wedding.*

round *adj.* shaped like a circle. *Our swimming pool is square, but theirs is round.*

  circular round like a circle. *The building has a circular tower.*

  ringlike like a circle. *The bracelet had ring-like links in it.*

sad *adj.* unhappy. *We were sad when our team lost.*

  joyless sad; without joy. *The joyless group waited for news about the fire.*

  unhappy sad; without cheer. *The clown wore a very unhappy face.*

sail *v.* to move swiftly, especially in air or on the water. *The ship can sail down the river.*

  boat to go in a boat. *We want to boat down the river to fish.*

  cruise to sail from place to place. *The ship will cruise to the islands.*

sand *n.* tiny bits of stone in large amounts, found in the desert and on shores along oceans, lakes, and rivers. *This beach has smooth sand.*

  dust fine, dry earth. *The dust settled all over the road.*

  grit fine bits of sand or gravel. *The boat was covered with grit.*

  powder dust made from grinding, crushing, or pounding a solid. *The rocks were ground into fine powder.*

scent *n.* an odor; a smell. *The dogs followed the scent of the wolf.*

  aroma strong odor; fragrance. *The aroma of flowers filled the air in the garden.*

  fragrance pleasant odor or smell. *The new fragrance smelled like fresh flowers.*

  smell an odor; a scent. *The smell of fresh bread filled the air.*

sharp *adj.* having a fine point or a thin edge for cutting. *The knife blade is sharp.*

  fine sharp. *The scissors had a very fine cutting edge.*

  keen sharp; cutting. *The knife had a keen edge.*

shoot *v.* to send out swiftly. *The archer will shoot an arrow at the target.*
  bombard to attack. *The children always bombard us with questions.*
  fire to shoot; discharge. *The officer tried to fire his gun at the target.*
  launch to send out; throw. *NASA will launch the rocket on schedule.*

sight *n.* something that is seen. *The sunset last night was a lovely sight.*
  scene view; picture. *The snow on the mountain peaks made a pretty scene.*
  spectacle sight; something to see. *The fireworks were a beautiful spectacle.*
  view something seen; scene. *She painted a scenic view of the hillside.*

sign *n.* something that stands for something else; symbol. *The sign for adding is +.*
  mark a symbol. *Writers put a question mark at the end of a question.*
  symbol something that stands for something else. *The + is a symbol used in math.*

sled *n.* a low platform on runners that slides over ice and snow. *It is fun to coast down a hill on a sled.*
  bobsled a long sled on runners with steering wheel and brakes. *He won an Olympic medal as brakeman for the second American bobsled.*
  sleigh cart on runners. *The horse pulled the sleigh over the snow.*

slow *adj.* not fast or quick. *The turtle makes slow but steady progress.*
  leisurely without hurry. *We took a leisurely stroll around town.*
  poky moving slowly. *The poky old camel took forever to get there.*
  antonym: fast

smooth *adj.* having no bumps or rough spots. *The smooth highway made driving a pleasure.*
  even level; flat. *The road is even with no holes or ruts.*
  level flat; even. *The grass was level as far as we could see.*
  antonym: rough

soft *adj.* quiet; gentle; mild. *She has a soft voice.*
  gentle low; soft. *He has a gentle way of playing the piano.*
  mild not harsh; not severe. *She had a very mild manner.*
  antonym: hard

soil *n.* ground; earth; dirt. *Plants grow in rich, dark soil.*
  dirt earth; soil. *We put some dirt into the flowerpot.*
  earth ground; soil. *Plant these seeds in black earth.*
  ground soil; earth. *The ground in the field is rich and fertile.*

splash *v.* to make wet or dirty. *The car tried to splash me with mud as it sped past.*
  splatter to splash. *The rain will splatter the windows.*
  sprinkle to scatter or spray with small drops. *Use the can to sprinkle water on the flowers.*

stick *n.* a long, thin piece of wood or other material. *We used a stick to stir the paint.*
  pole a long piece of wood. *The wires went to the telephone pole.*
  rod a thin stick. *The clothes were hung on a metal rod.*
  stake a stick pointed at one end. *The stake held up the corner of the tent.*

stop *v.* to halt or come to a halt. *The car will stop if we don't get more gas.*
  cease to come to an end; stop. *The treaty meant all fighting would cease.*
  halt to stop. *They had to halt the parade until the mayor arrived.*
  pause to stop for a short time. *We will pause for a short rest.*
  quit to stop. *The men quit working because of the rain.*

story *n.* a tale or account of an adventure or happening. *Mr. Lee told us a story about his grandfather.*
account a detailed statement about an event. *Each witness gave an account of the accident.*
legend a story of the past that might be based on real events. *The story of Robin Hood is a legend of old England.*
tale a made-up story. *The tale was about the magic of the sea creatures.*

street *n.* a road in a city or town. *This street is always crowded during rush hour.*
avenue a wide street. *Trees lined both sides of the avenue.*
boulevard a broad street. *The boulevard was named after a president.*
road a way for cars, trucks, etc., to travel. *The road went from town to the farm.*

summer *n.* the warmest season of the year. *Summer comes between spring and fall.*
midsummer the middle of the summer season. *The fair always came to town midsummer.*
summertime summer; the summer season. *We loved to swim in the summertime.*

sunshine *n.* the light from the sun. *Our cat loves to nap in the sunshine.*
sunlight the light of the sun. *The plants needed sunlight to grow.*

take *v.* to accept or receive; to grasp. *Take one; they're free.*
grab to seize suddenly; to take. *The man tried to grab the paper before it could fly away.*
grasp to hold; to seize. *She had to grasp the railing to walk down the stairs.*
seize to take hold of; to grasp. *He tried to seize the paper before we could read what it said.*
antonym: give

test *v.* to try; to examine; to put to a test. *Our teacher will test us in history next week.*
check to examine; to prove true or right. *The quiz will check how well we add numbers.*
examine to test skills or knowledge. *This assignment will examine your understanding of today's math lesson.*
quiz to give a short test. *The teacher needed to quiz the students on the chapter they had read.*

think *v.* to have in the mind as an opinion, idea, etc.; to believe. *She tried to think of the answer.*
believe to think something is true or real. *I believe you know the rules.*
expect to think something will occur. *I expect our team to win the game.*
imagine to picture in one's mind. *I like to imagine that elves did the work.*

track *n.* a mark or series of marks left by an animal, person, wagon, etc. *We saw a bicycle track in the snow.*
mark a line, spot, or dot made by something on an object. *That mark was made by the cat's claws.*
pattern a guide to make something. *Use the pattern to make the star.*

treat *v.* to handle; behave toward. *You must treat animals gently.*
handle to touch or use with the hands. *He meant to handle the vase carefully.*
manage to guide or handle. *She can manage the workers very well.*

under *prep.* below; beneath. *I found the money hidden under a rock.*
below lower than; under. *The sign is hanging below the branches.*
beneath below; under. *The light was placed beneath the window.*

until *prep.* up to the time of; till. *I slept until noon today.*
 till until; up to the time of. *The game lasted till five o'clock.*

very *adv.* greatly; extremely. *He was very unhappy when he lost his dog.*
 exceedingly unusually; greatly. *The report was done exceedingly well.*
 extremely greatly; strongly. *She was extremely busy at work today.*
 greatly in a great manner. *She was greatly pleased by the award.*

war *n.* a fight or struggle between countries or parts of a country. *There are great losses of life and destruction of property in a war.*
 fight a struggle; contest. *The fight was scheduled for Tuesday.*
 struggle a conflict; fight. *The struggle for freedom took many years.*

warm *v.* to make warm; to heat. *Warm the food before you serve it.*
 cook to prepare with heat. *The stew must cook for several hours.*
 heat to make or become warm. *The furnace will heat the house.*

wave *v.* to move up and down or from side to side. *The branches began to wave in the wind.*
 flap to move up and down. *The bird needed to flap its wings to get off the ground.*
 flutter to wave back and forth quickly. *The flag will flutter in the wind.*

wide *adj.* covering or having much space from side to side; broad; not narrow. *Our new car has wide seats.*
 broad large across; wide. *The broad road had four lanes in each direction.*
 extensive far-reaching; large. *There were extensive changes in the plans for the new building.*
 antonym: narrow

without *prep.* not having; with no. *I left without my umbrella.*
 less without; with something taken away. *The group was less two people.*
 minus less; decreased by. *Five minus two leaves three.*

woman *n.* a grown female person. *Your mother is a woman.*
 female woman; girl. *The new judge is a female.*
 lady a well mannered woman. *Everyone thinks of her as a real lady.*

work *n.* job; occupation; the thing one does to earn a living. *Her work is modeling clothes.*
 business work; occupation. *Their cleaning business can be found in the shopping mall.*
 job piece of work. *The plumber did a good job of fixing the shower.*
 occupation job; work. *Her occupation was bank manager.*

work *v.* to have a job for pay in order to make a living. *He likes to work in a big office.*
 labor to work hard; toil. *The gardener will have to labor many hours in the spring.*
 toil to work hard. *The farmer needs to toil in the field for many long hours.*

worry *n.* a cause of anxiety or trouble. *Money is a constant worry to him.*

anxiety fears about what might happen; worries. *She felt great anxiety over her test.*

nervousness anxiety; jumpiness. *His nervousness was caused by his fear of heights.*

wrap *v.* to enclose in something by winding or folding. *Wrap the baby in warm blankets.*

bundle up to wrap up. *He needed to bundle up in a heavy coat.*

envelop to wrap, cover, or hide. *The caterpillar will envelop itself in a cocoon.*